Malta

Berlitz®
Malta

Text by Lindsay Bennett
Photography: Pete Bennett
Cover photograph by Pete Bennett
Layout: Media Content Marketing, Inc.
Cartography by Raffaele De Gennaro
Managing Editor: Tony Halliday

Fourth Edition 2002

NO part of this book may be reproduced, stored in a retrieval system or transmitted in any form or means electronic, mechanical, photocopying, recording or otherwise, without prior written permission from Apa Publications. Brief text quotations with use of photographs are exempted for book review purposes only.

CONTACTING THE EDITORS

Every effort has been made to provide accurate information in this publication, but changes are inevitable. The publisher cannot be responsible for any resulting loss, inconvenience or injury. We would appreciate it if readers would call our attention to any errors or outdated information by contacting Berlitz Publishing, PO Box 7910, London SE1 1WE, England. Fax: (44) 20 7403 0290;
e-mail: berlitz@apaguide.demon.co.uk

CONTENTS

● A ☛ in the text denotes a highly recommended sight

Malta

THE ISLANDS AND
THE PEOPLE

T he tiny country of Malta sits at the heart of the Mediterranean Sea. Although only 316 sq kms (122 sq miles) in area, its land has felt the ebb and flow of the most influential ancient cultures, and its people have witnessed at first hand pivotal moments in European history. Settled as early as 5300 B.C. and coveted throughout its long history by the dominant power brokers of every age, Malta's amazing natural harbors have offered safety for some and contributed to disaster for others.

Seven islands comprise the country of Malta but only three are inhabited. Malta, the largest, is home to around 300,000 people, while Gozo (also known as Għawdex) has a fifth of this population on an island a quarter of the size. Comino has only a handful of houses with no motorized vehicles, and the two St. Paul's Bay islands see only day visitors. Finally, there is tiny Filfla, which witnesses only the footsteps of birds and lizards — it's a nature reserve, and no human visitors are allowed.

Malta is almost equidistant between Gibraltar at the western mouth of the Mediterranean, and the coast of the Holy Land and the Suez Canal in the east. It lies 560 kms (350 miles) from the African coast, and only 100 kms (62 miles) from Sicily at the foot of Italy. It fact, it was attached to Sicily until the end of the last ice age when sea levels rose and washed in to part the islands.

Geologically, the land of Malta is made up of layers of sandstone and limestone; a porous structure that has been eroded over the millennia by the power of wind and water. Hundreds of narrow coves have been cut into the coastline, interspersed with high cliffs and a few sandy bays. Underground, there are numerous cave systems with impressive stalactites and stalagmites produced by mineral rich water droplets dripping incessantly for millions of years. Ancient watercourses once flowed across the Maltese landscape, and these supported populations of hippopotamuses and elephants — hundreds of fossilized skeletons have been found at Għar Dalam in the east of Malta. Today the rivers have dried up, so Malta relies on winter rainfall, as well as a technologically advanced desalinization process for its water supply. After warm spring showers, the cliffs and rural waysides are awash with wild grasses and a plethora of pretty flowers; birdsong rings out across the ripening crops and breezes play on the water. During the dry summer months the hillsides grow parched and brown; the air is hot and still, and only the constant sound of the cicada (the Mediterranean's ubiquitous noisy insect) breaks the silence.

Settlers arrived here from Sicily as early as 5300 B.C. They were a farming people; independent and self-sufficient. However, as soon as seafaring allowed greater mobility, Malta became an important port on the developing shipping routes, and this began a long tradition of control from abroad by the dominant maritime power of each successive era. Over time these shores were visited or settled by Phoenicians, Ancient Greeks, Romans and Arabs; each people have left their mark. Later, numerous European feudal overlords extended temporary jurisdiction here. They saw Malta as little more than an asset to be stripped for short-term gain. In the 16th century Malta was leased to The Order of St John, a military order of Knights Hospitallers, who had tried unsuccessfully to defend Jerusalem against the Muslims. Under their dominion, Malta became arguably the most fortified place in the world. Their capital, Valletta, is now a masterpiece of late Medieval and Baroque archi-

On a typically sun-drenched day, a son helps his father to harvest onions in preparation for the market.

tecture. The French evicted the Knights from their fortifications two hundred years later, but they in turn soon yielded to the British, who then ruled the islands — with some limited self-determination for its inhabitants — until 1964, when Malta gained independence.

And what of the people who have lived so many centuries under the rule of foreign powers? They are some of the most welcoming people you could ever hope to meet. In A.D. 60 when St. Paul arrived unexpectedly on the island as the result of a shipwreck, he received a warm welcome from the people, just as visitors do today. As you study your map while sightseeing, you are sure to be approached by someone offering their help with directions, or suggestions about where to visit.

Throughout the years, the Maltese have remained faithful to their own traditions and have a unique culture and language. Most of the local people speak Malti, the national language that is closely related to Arabic. However, they also have English as a second official language, and Italian and French are widely spoken as well. Consequently, communication is never a problem when you are traveling around the islands.

The Maltese and Gozitans (the people of Gozo) have a fierce loyalty to what they hold dear. Their Catholic faith is an anchor in their lives, and the pride of every village or town is its large, highly decorated church. Family relationships are close, and everyone displays a respect for the older members of society.

Perhaps greatest of all is a love of their island, for which they fought so bravely during WWII that Great Britain awarded them its highest award for civil bravery, the George Cross, in 1942. They are proud of their independence, having one of the highest electoral turnouts in the world. Over

Fishing boats rest up in preparation for their next tour of duty in a quay adjoining Spinola point.

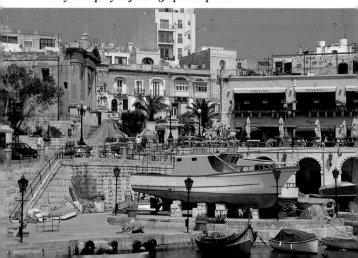

95% of the eligible population exercise their right to vote and they are vociferous in their opinions on the way forward for their country.

The Maltese, of course, don't spend all their time in such serious and earnest pursuits: They very much enjoy their relaxed island lifestyle. Whether it is a fisherman mending his nets or keeping his *luzzu* boat spic-and-span, or the waiter calmly going about his business at the harbor side restaurant, there's an unhurried air that helps the visitor to relax too.

Everyone knows everyone else and there's still a comforting network of mutual support here. A favorite pastime is to stroll along the promenade or along Republic Street taking in the cool evening air. If there's a new baby to show off, you'll find both Grandmas proudly pushing the carriage, basking in the attention and warm congratulations of their neighbors.

On Sundays whole families get together for a picnic or long lunch at mamma's. After eating, the children play noisily while the adults sit around the table discussing the topic of the day.

The best place to meet Maltese and Gozitan people is at the village *festa*, where the parish saint's day is celebrated. Work comes to a complete standstill as the whole population comes out to follow the saint's statue in a somber parade around the village and offer prayers of thanks in church, before breaking out the band and fireworks for a huge celebratory party.

Although tradition still plays an important part in daily life, Malta has experienced a great deal of change since independence. Tourism has become the focus of wealth creation at a time of major population growth, making Malta one of the most densely populated countries in Europe. Both of these situations have led to a building boom, which has on the one hand provided modern homes for families and accommodations for visitors, but has also put pressure on

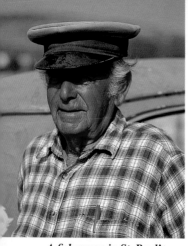

A fisherman in St. Paul's Bay ponders what the sea holds in store for him.

farmland and fishing communities. Much of the new construction has not been of the most tasteful variety, and a preponderance of concrete blights most of Malta's resorts (though Gozo has made the smarter decision, opting to carry on building in traditional sandstone).

The islands also have so much history — it's sown into the fabric of almost every Maltese building — that the accompanying responsibility can be problematic. Many historic buildings have pending development plans earmarked for them, but these are expensive and investment is finite; meanwhile, castles and forts sit sad and careworn. It doesn't mean that there is a disdain for history, simply that there is almost too much here for one small country to cope with.

Malta is a popular vacation destination with an organized tourist infrastructure. There are warm, clear waters for swimming, snorkelling, and diving; footpaths and farm tracks for hiking, cycling, and horse riding; and guaranteed hot sunshine between May and October. The islands have many loyal devotees who vacation here year after year. They return because, although it has touches of the exotic, Malta has much that feels safe, familiar, and comfortable. They also know that they are guaranteed the welcome reserved for a friend, the welcome that the Maltese extend to all their visitors.

A BRIEF HISTORY

S itting at the heart of the Mediterranean Sea, Malta has long been seen by power brokers as an important piece of land. It has played a key role in many of the world's major power struggles and has often been at the center of key events in the history of Europe.

Civilization dawned on the islands long before recorded history and the islands are rich in sites to explore. Settlers arrived on Malta, at the earliest, around 5200 B.C., well after the end of the Ice Age raised sea levels and separated the island from Sicily. They were farmers and brought wheat and a range of domestic animals with them. Archeologists theorize that it was during this first wave of settlement that Malta lost all of its native forest.

It took almost another millennium for any great cultural development to take place, yet when it did, Malta saw the flowering of a sophisticated society, with a high level of building skills and complex rituals surrounding burial of the dead. The Żeebuġ phase of the Megalithic period (4100–3800 B.C.) saw extensive construction of religious sites which have been excavated and studied in the 20th century and are open to the public today. The basic architectural forms found appear in such enormous stone temples as Ggantija on Gozo and Ħaġar Qim (hah-jahr-khEEM) on Malta.

Some of the most magnificent prehistoric buildings were the temples of the Tarxien period (about 3200 to 2500 B.C.), named after the place where several of them are located. These are a stunning feat of construction for a supposedly primitive society. After them, the building of temples came to a sudden end, possibly as a result of invasion, though other theories suggest a plague or the pressures of overpopulation.

What is clear is that a new wave of immigrants arrived from what is now southern Italy. Known as the "Cemetery People," they used the Tarxien temples as a burial ground but left only fragmentary traces of their culture. Far more relics have survived from the era of their Bronze Age successors, who built fortified villages — including Borġ in-Nadur (borj in nah-DOOR), where the defensive wall dating from 1500 B.C. is still visible.

Carthage and Rome

By the 9th century B.C., Phoenician sailors from the eastern Mediterranean had reached the Maltese islands. They established a colony at Carthage in North Africa that grew into a great trading republic, dominating the entire region. Inscriptions, coins and tombs remain as a record of their control in Malta.

Greek civilization was another strong influence. Although they did not settle the island, they had colonies in nearby Sicily and there was frequent contact between the island cultures.

When a new power, Rome, began to expand southwards, a clash with Carthage was inevitable. During the three Punic Wars between these two powers, from 264 to 146 B.C., the Carthaginians were finally defeated. Malta was taken by a Roman expedition in 218 B.C. under the command of the consul Tiberius Sempronius. The Romans took over the Carthaginian capital — where Mdina now stands — fortifying it and building luxurious villas elsewhere in Malta. You can see the remains of a Roman house between Mdina and Rabat.

In A.D. 60, one of Malta's most important historical events occurred. St. Paul and St. Luke were shipwrecked just off the island, somewhere in the area now known as St. Paul's Bay.

The historic Mnajdra Temple on Malta gives us a fascinating insight into pre-Roman ways of life.

They had been traveling as prisoners from Caesarea to Rome, where Paul was to appeal to Caesar for justice.

Both men spent the winter months in a cave at Mdina–Rabat, where St. Paul preached the gospel. His message and the miracles that he performed began the conversion of the islanders to Christianity. One of the first converts was the Roman governor, Publius, who was eventually named the first Bishop of Malta. Malta is considered to be the first Christian "country" in the world, and remains fundamentally Christian to the present day.

Arabs and Crusaders

As the Roman Empire went into decline, it was divided into western and eastern sections. Malta was allocated to the east, governed from Constantinople. However, control of the furthest reaches of the empire proved difficult and various tribes squabbled over the island. Arab influence grew as Roman power declined, and they became the new rulers in A.D. 870. One of their first actions was to build a fortified citadel at Mdina.

Although the Arabs tolerated Christianity, many islanders emigrated, and some remaining Maltese converted to Islam. Raiding parties taking men and women into slavery further decimated the population. For protection, Maltese villages developed inland rather than in defenseless coastal locations.

Two centuries of Arab rule left an indelible impression on Malta and especially on the language. Cotton and citrus

Valletta's city walls merge here with St. Elmo, a fort built to protect Malta from Turkish invaders in the 16th century.

fruits were introduced and became the mainstay of the economy as trade expanded.

However, quarrels among the Arabs eventually weakened the islands' defenses, and the Norman Count, Roger I of Sicily, saw a chance to improve his strategic position. After his successful invasion in 1090, the island became part of the Kingdom of Sicily.

Malta was a key link in the line of communication during the Crusades, while passing first through the hands of several feudal European lords before being taken by the Aragonese in 1283. It was at this time that the Maltese nobility began to develop. In 1397 a system of local government called the Università was established and several local families became fundamental in its development.

Despite increasing autonomy, the island was exploited by overseas feudal lords, who were interested in Malta mainly as a source of revenue. The Maltese worked at commerce, farming and piracy in order to earn the taxes demanded of them.

In 1428 Malta was declared a royal domain by King Alphonso of Spain, cutting out the feudal landlords. However, this could not protect Malta from repeated attacks by Turkish raiders and pirates from North Africa. By the 16th century, with Spain's attention now completely drawn to the New World, morale in Malta was low and the economy was in decline.

The Knights of St. John

The 16th century saw the Mediterranean Sea becoming increasingly dominated by the Ottoman Turks led by their Sultan, Suleiman the Magnificent. Their chief adversaries, the crusading Knights of the Order of St. John, had long since been expelled from the Holy Land, yet still held onto a base on the island of Rhodes off the coast of Turkey. After repeated attacks and a six-month siege in 1522, the Turks took Rhodes on New Year's Day 1523. Surprisingly, Suleiman was merciful and granted the Knights leave to go. While they were adrift again, they departed with their wealth intact. Philippe Villiers de l'Isle Adam, the courageous Grand Master of the Order, led his soldiers from their home to Sicily and Italy, and eight years without a base. Eventually, Charles V, Holy Roman Emperor offered the island of Malta to them and in 1530, the grand master and his 4,000 men moved to this new base.

The knights set about building fortifications and living quarters on the coast at Birgu (later called Vittoriosa) and the neighboring peninsula, Senglea. As the Grand Harbor area became the focus of activity, so the importance of the old capital, Mdina, declined. When the Spanish Inquisition arrived on the island in 1561, they made a home in this new capital, putting the Church's seal of approval on the city.

The knights had not seen the last of the Turks, however. Suleiman regretted his charitable act and, soon after the knights arrived in Malta, was plotting to take over the island because of its strong strategic position. Th e Knights also found themselves threatened by North African pirates, under the command of one Dragut. They devastated the island of Gozo in 1546 and took thousands of Gozitans as slaves in 1551. When Dragut then joined forces with the rampaging Turks, the future looked bleak for the defenders of Christendom.

The Great Siege

When word reached Grand Master Jean Parisot de la Valette of a huge force approaching his island, he sent out desperate appeals for help. Only a few volunteers came. On 19 May

1565, a Turkish fleet of 138 galleys disembarked an army of 38,000 at Marsaxlokk Bay. Among them were 4,000 fanatical janissaries, mostly converts to Islam, the crack troops of their time.

The invaders, commanded by Admiral Piali and Mustapha Pasha, were confident of victory. De la Valette had only his 600 knights, 9,000 other troops and eight galleys, but these men proved astoundingly resilient, as they were to perform one of the most valiant defenses in history.

Throughout the summer of 1565, heat, disease, and dwindling food supplies plagued both sides as they battled on. The Maltese people fought and suffered along with the knights in fierce resistance. Each man lost was irreplaceable, and strategic positions were abandoned one by one for lack of troops to hold them. At one critical point, even de la Valette himself (though he was 72) threw himself into the fray, inspiring his followers by his courage. Despite their advantage, the valiant defenders slowly wore down the Turks. Arguments between Turk commanders did not help. In one assault

The 'Second Great Siege' monument honors Malta's sacrifice in World War II.

This cannon was once an integral part of the defences overlooking Fort St. Elmo.

alone on Senglea, the Turks lost 2,500 men.

At last, reinforcements for the besieged were mustered by the Sicilian viceroy, Garcia de Toledo, and on 7 September they landed at Mellieha Bay. The Turks were fooled into believing the fresh troops to be more numerous than they really were, and they lifted the siege. As the remnant of their forces sailed away, their defeat marked the turning point in Ottoman fortunes, and their Empire began a slow spiral of decline. In Malta there was great rejoicing, though the island was devastated by the siege.

Money poured in from grateful Christian monarchs around Europe, relieved to have been saved from the threat of further Muslim expansion. Plans were drawn up for a new city to the west of Birgu, on the Sceberras peninsula between the two long harbors, since this position could be more easily defended in any future conflict. The Order obtained the services of the grateful Pope's own architect, Laparelli. The capital was to be called Valletta — named after the resolute de la Valette (the double L results from the Italian version of his name). Its modern design allowed for easy movement — straight streets — and cooling sea breezes, something lacking in the design of medieval Birgu. The plan of the city inspired Maltese architect Gerolamo Cassar. He is responsible for much of the way Valletta looks today, with large fine buildings and harmonious styles that blend early Baroque with classical elements.

By the 18th century, however, much of the Mediterranean was in the doldrums. New trade routes to the riches of the East, around the Cape of Good Hope, and from the Americas and the Caribbean brought new cargoes, and consequently took all the best investment. Without their old enemies, the Ottoman Turks, to fight against, the order itself seemed to lose its focus, becoming dissolute and tired. The French Revolution of 1789, and the subsequent downfall of the aristocracy and the church in France, shook the order to the core, for it deprived the knights of much of their support — and most of their revenue.

Enter Napoleon

In 1798, Napoleon eyed the Mediterranean with avarice and came to the same conclusion reached by many commanders before and since: Malta would be valuable to him, and it would pose a serious threat if it were to fall into the hands of his enemies. On 10 June he invaded, landing at Valletta, and presented the knights with a simple order: They must pack up and leave. Where others had failed, Napoleon succeeded. Grand Master von Hompesch had no stomach for a fight and simply did as he was ordered. After 268 years in residence, the world's most famous military order departed without any action to defend their stronghold.

Two years of French rule followed, in which the arrogant behavior of the occupiers made them hated by both the Maltese and the Church. A popular insurrection began, and

Winston Churchill is immortalized by a bust in Valletta's Upper Barracca Gardens.

troops sent by the King of Naples joined the Maltese. At the same time the French were at war with the British and, following a series of disastrous naval engagements against British Admiral Horatio Nelson, they capitulated in 1800. The 1802 Treaty of Amiens gave Malta back to the Order of St. John, but the Maltese protested and the knights stayed away.

Malta's value as a naval base now came to the attention of the British, who had recently relinquished Menorca. Great Britain informally administered the islands for the remainder of the ongoing Napoleonic Wars and British possession was formally recognized in the Treaty of Paris in 1814, and again at the Congress of Vienna.

British Colony

In 1813 — a year marked by a plague that killed off a fifth of Malta's inhabitants — Sir Thomas Maitland arrived as governor. Nicknamed "King Tom," he dismissed the traditional self-governing Università and introduced sweeping reforms to bring the legal system into line with the English one. A period of stability followed which saw new crops introduced, more vineyards planted, and water resources better managed, resulting in increased crop yields. The building of bases for the Royal Navy who patrolled the expanding British Empire gave a boost to employment and prosperity. The opening of the Suez Canal in 1869 increased Mediterranean shipping, and by 1880 Grand Harbor was a major port.

The Maltese, however, had not lost their desire for independence, and during the 19th century a succession of constitutions gave the people varying degrees of autonomy. Riots following World War I brought about real change, codified in the new Constitution of 1921. The Maltese became responsible for their own internal affairs, while London retained control of defense, foreign affairs, and matters affecting the Empire.

The Second Great Siege

Malta was vital to the Allied cause during World War II. Not only could ships and aircraft based here block the deployment of Italy's navy, they could also attack Axis supply routes to the German and Italian forces operating from North Africa. When Italy entered the war in June 1940, its first move was to bomb Malta. During 1941, Italian, and later German, aircraft kept up almost incessant raids.

As Rommel advanced through Egypt in the spring of 1942, air attacks increased, and in March and April the islands were hit with more than twice the weight of bombs that fell on London during any *full year* of the war. Life became increasingly miserable on Malta, with people living in cellars and caves in conditions of near-starvation.

This second great siege was only relieved in August 1942 with the arrival of a convoy of ships packed with fuel and essential supplies. Only five ships out of the original 13 made it from London, but it was enough to save the island and the allied foothold in the area.

The price of freedom, however, had been high: thousands of people killed or injured, and thousands of homes destroyed. In recognition of the bravery and sacrifice shown by the Maltese, the island was awarded Britain's highest honor for civilian courage — the George Cross. To this day it appears on the national flag.

Independence

After the war, Britain gave Malta financial assistance for reconstruction, and a new constitution granted the islands self-government within the Commonwealth. Plans for the complete transfer of power met with difficulties, but on 21 September 1964, Malta became fully independent for the

Malta's seafaring culture stands on proud display at Dockyard Creek in Vittoriosa.

first time in recorded history. Her parliament declared a republic in 1974.

In 1979, British forces bade farewell to the island. Although the islanders welcomed independence, many had depended on the British services either directly or indirectly for their livelihood, and the island quickly needed to find other forms of revenue.

Tourism seemed to be a perfect choice. The natural warmth of the people and the climate, along with the wealth of historical buildings, would guarantee visitors, and Malta benefited from an explosion in European air travel in the 1970s and 1980s. This rush to develop a tourist infrastructure has not always resulted in the best-planned or prettiest modern resorts, but in the 1990s Malta began to make efforts to do justice to their older architectural beauty. Innovative tourism ventures, five star resorts, and a new cruise port planned in the early part of this new millennium are sure to reinforce Malta's position as a prime tourist destination.

Politically, however, the people have a more interesting debate to settle. In 1995, Malta applied for entry into the European Union, but recent developments have proven that this is by no means a cut and dried issue. The 1996 Maltese elections resulted in a change of policy and a freeze on the application, followed by another election in 1998 that called for a thawing of the frozen process. Having undergone the "screening" process that identifies areas of discrepancy between Maltese and EU laws in early 2000, a final decision is expected by the end of 2002. At present, though, whether they will allow the surrender of newly won and greatly enjoyed independence in favor of embracing the greater Europe can only be a matter of speculation. Only time will tell.

WHERE TO GO

The Maltese islands are compact and relatively easy to explore either independently, in a rental car, on public transport, or by an organized tour. We'll begin by looking at the largest island, Malta — including the capital Valletta, followed by the settlements around Valletta and the Grand Harbor. Other sections of the book will explore the south east coast before moving to the main settlements inland. Finally we'll journey along the north coast before sailing across the water to Comino and Gozo, Malta's other inhabited islands.

VALLETTA

When the Knights of St. John first settled on Malta they made their home at Birgu, on the eastern side of Grand Harbor. Directly in their line of sight was the Sceberras Peninsula, jutting out between the Grand Harbor and Marsamxett (Mar-sam-shett) Harbor. Here they built a fort called St. Elmo. During the Great Siege of 1565 the Turks took the Sceberras Peninsula and the fort, inflicting great damage on the knights from across the harbor. Following the knights' final triumph, it was decided that they would move their headquarters onto the peninsula. Plans were made to rebuild Fort St. Elmo and to create a great citadel to house the knights. This citadel was to be called Valletta. Work began in 1566 from plans drawn up by Francesco Laparelli, architect to the Vatican and the Medici family. He promised that the city could be constructed in a mere three months, but when he returned to Italy two years later there was still a great deal to be done. The project was left in the hands of his Maltese assistant Gerolamo Cassar who finished the work, and added his own imprint on the finished city.

Here we see the view of Valletta and the Grand Harbor from Ricasoli Point, itself a noted historical landmark.

The simple yet effective design was brilliantly formatted. High thick **walls** on all sides with **bastions** at regular intervals and two Cavaliers to mark the main entrance. At the outward tip Fort St. Elmo, separated from the rest of the town by a deep ditch, would form a final line of defense should Valetta ever be overrun. A series of long straight streets divided the town with interconnecting streets forming a grid pattern. This would allow for quick movement of troops through the citadel during hostilities, and bring cooling sea breezes into the heart of the city, even in the oppressive heat of summer. Water remained a difficulty, but later, in the early part of the 17th century, Grand Master Alof de Wignacourt planned and constructed an aqueduct from Mdina that guaranteed a supply to the extent that fountains and gardens could be added to beautify Valletta.

Today, though Valletta has moved on into modern times, the initial *raison d'être* for the creation of the city can still clearly be seen. The walls, bastions, and fort still stand strong; and to see the city from the air, or from the waters of the Grand Harbor or Marsamxett Harbor, really brings home the amazing feat of the builders. You can walk around the walls in about 90 minutes. Now that enemy raids are a thing of the past, all you need to bring is a camera to capture the wonderful views they offer.

> Take a siesta in the afternoon.

The interior of the city was marked by the building of a series of large *auberges* where each different group of knights or *langue* (see page 56) lived in commune. To these were added convents and churches and a huge hospital to treat the sick. Following the departure of the knights at the end of the 18th century, many of these beautiful buildings were taken for other civil or military uses, and Valletta's streets became home to thousands of people, living in high-rise (three and four story) buildings decorated with wooden balcony windows. Lines of these balconies — undulating with the rise and fall of streets and stairways — are one of the enduring images of the city, and of all settlements around Malta.

Valletta is less than one kilometer (1/3 mile) wide and 1.5km (9/10 mile) long. It is best visited on foot, allowing you to take in every detail of the architecture and to explore the quiet nooks and crannies.

The main entrance to Valletta, **City Gate**, cuts the old walls, but it has little architectural value. Because it leads to the main bus station for the island, it is always busy with people and stalls selling cool drinks and snacks. The gate sits at the top of the main arterial route through the city, **Triq il-Republikka** (Republic Street), and exploring its attractions makes a good start for your tour. The upper section is relatively flat, then drops down towards Fort St. Elmo to the north. Republic Street is a wide pleasant thoroughfare with many fine buildings. It also has shops and cafes for you to enjoy and you will find a tourist information office immediately through City Gate on your right.

Strolling down the street, which was known as Strada Reale during the knights' days and Kingsway under British rule, you will first notice the ruins of what would have been a large building; vestiges of classical columns can still be seen. This was the site of the **Royal Opera House**, which was bombed in 1942 and never rebuilt. Further along on your left, you will find the Auberge de Provence finished in 1575 and now housing the **Archaeological Museum**. The building itself is interesting, being one of the auberges that the public can still enter, but the collections that it displays are also fascinating and add lots of extra detail to the bare bones of dates and eras in Malta's long history. On the first floor, the Neolithic and Bronze Ages are brought to life. Beautiful pottery effigies — including the Rubenesque Venus of Malta — and stone carvings found at Tarxien and other sites bear witness to the sophistication of these ancient peoples. A timeline near the doorway points out that the Maltese temple sites were constructed over 1,000 years

What's in a Name?

The origin of Malta's name has often been debated. The most plausible theories are that it is either a corruption of the Phoenician *malat* (meaning "safe harbor"), or that it comes from the Greek *meli* (the word for "honey"), a famous product of the islands in early times.

Gozo (or Ghawdex, pronounced "Ow-dehsh") is probably derived from the Greek *gaudos*, which in turn comes from the Phoenician for a small boat.

St. John's Co-Cathedral was built and named for the order's patron saint, who ruled Malta for 300 years.

before the pyramids in Egypt, and are the oldest free-standing structures so far discovered in the world. Upstairs, the collection moves on to more recent history, featuring finds from the Roman era.

Walk along to the Law Courts, built after World War II on the site of the Auberge d'Auvergne. They sit looking out at the austere flank of one of the most important buildings in Valletta, the **Co-Cathedral of St. John** dedicated by the knights to the patron saint of their order. Turn right here on St. John's Street to find its main entrance. Cassar designed the church, constructed between 1573–1577, and his plan surrounded the building with a number of small open squares, much needed areas of relaxation in today's crowded city. The severe façade of the church belies the ornate beauty within — it is a Baroque masterpiece. Small chapels off the main nave are dedicated to each langue, and the floor is replete with tombs of knights, highly decorated with colored marble. The vault is decorated with several huge canvasses by Mattia Preti (1613–1690) — an Italian artist favored by the order during his lifetime — featuring scenes from the life of St. John the Baptist, which would act as a focal point for praying knights in centuries past. The church, granted Co-Cathedral status by Pope Pius VII in 1816 (the main cathedral remained St. Paul's in Mdina), also has an interesting museum with beautiful Flemish tapestries and other works of art. It also displays vestments and early religious books.

Beyond the Cathedral on Republic Street you will find a small square now called **Republic Square**, which has at its center a rather solemn statue of Queen Victoria, usually sporting a pigeon on top of her tiny crown. In fine weather, she is surrounded by a sea of parasols, and tables put out by nearby cafes where you can enjoy lunch or a drink and watch the world go by. The buildings on the square are beautifully colonnaded but the eye is drawn to a very ornate façade on the eastern flank. This fine neo-classical building, the last to be constructed by the Knights, was finished in 1796. It was originally intended to house the large collection of books owned by the order, designated as a *Bibliotheca Publica* (Public Library) in 1760, and is now called the **National Library**. For those with a particular interest in the Knights of St. John, the library is a treasure trove of information and artifacts. In addition to a large collection of books, including over 46 printed before 1500, there are a number of charters and documents relating to the workings of the order, including the original Deed of Donation of Malta to the order in 1530.

The first floor of the library building, underneath the colonnades, has long been the home of Café Premier, a meeting place

The Queen Victoria monument at Republic Square is surrounded by cafés.

for coffee and romantic trysts. In the late 1990s the cafe was totally refurbished and is now a smart patisserie. Next door is **The Great Siege of Malta and The Knights of St. John Experience**, the most recent addition to Valetta's attractions. This walk-through exhibition charts the history of the order from their earliest days in Jerusalem, to staging points in Cyprus and Rhodes before their arrival in Malta. It then brings to life the fight with the Ottoman Turks and the building of Valletta. Life size figures depict the major characters involved and you travel through Suleiman's court, on an Ottoman ship bringing soldiers to fight the knights, and then enter the battlefield itself. The displays are enhanced by a well-produced, synchronized soundtrack and film re-enactments. The attraction has the patronage of the present Grand Master of the Order of St. John.

Next to the Republic Square is the huge façade of the **Magisterial Palace** or **Grand Master's Palace**, once the official and private residence of the Grand Master of the Knights of St. John. The palace, with its hundred meter long façade, was constructed between 1572 and 1580 with one entrance arch (nearest Archbishop Street). Later in the 18th century Grand Master Pinto added the second entrance and the long balconies that grace each corner. Today the palace is used as the seat of the Maltese Parliament and the presidential office but a large part of the palace can be toured depending on the legislative timetable.

On the first floor is the **Armoury collection**, much of which dates from around the time of the Great Siege in the mid-16th century (Napoleon took the 18th century arms with him when he left the island. These would have been state of the art at the time). A rare hide and copper cannon can be seen, along with pikes, shields and a large collection of armor, including Grand Master Wignacourt's dress suite, highly decorated with gilt.

On the first floor, the **State Chambers** reveal a great deal about the wealth and power of the knights at their zenith. The Council Hall was where the day-to-day activities would be discussed. Today this room is known as the Tapestry Chamber because of the large Gobelin Tapestries that adorn the walls. This room also served as a meeting room for the Maltese legislature from 1921 until 1975.

The Banqueting Hall was badly damaged during World War II but has been completely renovated. It is adorned with portraits including those of several British monarchs.

The Great Council Chambers was the main Hall of State. It housed meetings with visiting dignitaries and overseas knights, and was the

If it's armor you want, the Armory at the Grand Master's Palace is hard to beat.

forum for discussing matters of state and foreign affairs. The hall is beautifully decorated with a frieze depicting scenes from the Great Siege of 1565. The former Grand Master's Throne sits on a raised platform under the coat of arms of the Republic of Malta. It is now used as the Chair of State of the country.

Just beyond the Great Council Chamber is the Ambassador's Room where foreign envoys were received. The room serves the same purpose to this day.

From the entrance of The Magisterial Palace, look across the small square to find the **Malta War Experience**. This multimedia mixture of film and still photo footage tells the story of Malta during World War II. All the footage is original and brings home the tremendous damage done to the buildings, as well as the fear suffered by the people.

North of the palace, Republic Street drops down from the top of the ridge of the Sceberras Peninsula towards Fort St.

Elmo. A series of wide shallow marble steps flank the roadway here. Be careful, because they can be slippery in wet weather. At No. 74 Republic Street you will find **Casa Rocca Piccola**, a house built in the 16th century by a noble family, which is still a family home today. The interior is an archetypal example of house design at the time, including an interior court-

At the entrance to Fort St. Elmo, Palace Guards still keep a watchful eye.

yard with stairs leading to a *piano nobile* or second floor living area. The rooms are full of antique furniture including a beautiful portable chapel that folds neatly into a chest of drawers for traveling.

The northern section of Valletta is given over to family homes, so you will pass through an area of playing children and darting cats, before reaching **Fort St. Elmo**. This huge fortification — pride of the Knights of St. John — was rebuilt and extended after being overrun in the siege of 1565 and was further fortified in 1687. The large holes on the forecourt of the fort are the entrances to huge underground grain stores, each of which could hold 5,000 tons of food. Flat stones shield the openings against rain and provide a safety for modern visitors against the danger of falling into the stores. The fort, which was upgraded several times during British rule, last saw action during World War II and shows evidence of almost every era of its existence. It is open on weekends and holds a regular **In Guardia!** re-enactment (see page 88).

> Cover shoulders when you enter churches. Men should wear long trousers.

Vendome Bastion, a part of the fort once used to store gunpowder is now the **National War Museum**. Enter through an arch some 50 m west of the main castle entrance. The museum, dedicated in 1975, tells the story of Malta's second great siege in World War II, and her role in the Allies' eventual success in 1945. Photographs show the devastation caused by Axis bombing and relate the stories of heroism by Maltese nationals and servicemen alike. Hundreds of relics are on view, from the Gloucester Gladiator biplane "Faith" — one of only four on hand to protect the island at the start of hostilities — to ration books and gas masks. Pride of place goes to the **George Cross**, awarded to Malta in 1942 in recognition of the islands' bravery in the face of continued Axis attacks. It is displayed in a glass case lined with velvet.

Now that we have explored the attractions along Republic Street, we can head out to the other parts of the city. The attractions are not difficult to find on the narrow streets, and we'll look first at those on the streets to the left of Republic Street (Marsamxett side), then to the right (Grand Harbor side).

On South Street at the City Gate end of Republic Street is the **National Museum of Fine Arts**, housed in the residence of knight Jean de Soubrian, which was completed in 1571. During British rule it was the residence of the Naval Commander in Chief, a very important military position. The building is interesting in itself, with a stairway decorated in an ornamental Baroque style. The museum has 24 rooms displaying a range of European art. Two rooms are given over to the works of Mattia Preti, the hallways are used to display a range of temporary exhibitions, and the remaining rooms feature Maltese artists, with many landscape paintings. Portraits of several Grand Masters were painted by Antoine de Favray (1706–1798). A curious collection of knight's memorabilia can be found in the basement. These include coins, religious relics, and model ships.

As the threat of the Turks subsided, the knights began to look for worldly pleasures to fill their time and in 1731, the then Grand Master, Manoel de Vilhena commissioned a theater to be built in the city. **The Manoel Theatre** opened a year later and held regular performances until the Royal Opera House opened in 1861. The Manoel fell into disrepair though it was used for performances in 1881 and between the wars. In 1960, it was refurbished at government expense, and today its beautifully decorated stalls and elliptical ceiling are well worth seeing. There are regular guided tours so you don't need to wait for a performance. Seaward of the theater, and dom-

A recently renovated Carmelite church spruces up the Valletta skyline as seen from Marsamxett harbour.

inating the Valletta skyline, is the **Carmelite Church,** which was completed in 1958 on the site of a Cassar-designed church that was badly damaged during World War II. The dome is 73 m (240 ft) high and capped with a layer of Malta sandstone to match the city walls.

A number of interesting buildings sit to the Grand Harborside of Republic Street (the right). If you enter the city by car you will find yourself facing one of the most beautiful historic buildings of Valletta. The **Auberge de Castille**, built in 1574, was home to knights from Castille, Leon and Portugal. Grand Master Emanuel Pinto De Fonseca added the beautifully ornamented façade in 1744 in the fashionable Baroque style of the time. The auberge now acts as the prime minister's office, and although it is probably the most photographed building in the city, there is no public access.

Upper Barracca Gardens,
once privy to the few, are
now an ideal public space.

From the auberge, head right, and to the left of a small Greek revival style structure — the Malta Stock Exchange — to **Upper Barracca Gardens**, once a private garden of the knights but today offering local people and visitors alike the most spectacular views of the Grand Harbor. The Gardens sit on the ramparts of St. Peter and St. Paul Bastion and were laid out in the 17th century. Numerous plaques and sculptures adorn the flower beds but most people head out to the balcony, camera in hand, to watch boats entering the harbor and to look to the "three cities" across the bay. You have clear views of boats in the huge Malta Dry Docks, and the walls of Fort St. Angelo at the Knights original headquarters at Vittoriosa.

Walking north along St. Paul Street you will find the narrow façade of **St. Paul's Shipwreck Church**. Designed by Cassar, this is one of the oldest churches in Valletta, and has several paintings by Attilio Palombi depicting scenes from the saint's life. A large wooden statue adorns the interior and the church safeguards two important religious relics, an arm bone said to be that of the saint, and a piece of the column on which he was allegedly beheaded.

Back on the city wall at the Grand Harbor side (from St. Paul's Street travel down several flights of stairs towards the Poste de Castille) is **Lower Barracca Gardens**. This also offers a view across the harbor to Vittoriosa, but gives a different perspective of the upper gardens with a vista of Ricasoli Point at the eastern mouth of Grand Harbor. In the center of the gardens is a Doric Temple erected as a memorial to Sir Alexander Ball, who led the Maltese insurrection against the French at the start of the 19th century.

> Please – jek joghg bok (jehek yoy-bok)

Walking along the city wall towards Fort St. Elmo will bring you to the huge **Bell of Remembrance**, tolled every day at noon for the Maltese lost during World War II. From the bell you can clearly see the long plain façade of the **Sacra Infermeria**, the hospital run by the Knights — one of the most advanced medical facilities of its day when it opened in 1574. It was used as a medical facility until after World War I. The large wards — the longest was 161 m (528 ft) — now house the Mediterranean Conference Center, one of Malta's success stories since independence, which hosts several major international conferences each year. Also housed in the Infermeria is **The Malta Experience**, a multimedia spectacular which takes viewers on a 50 minute journey through the history of the islands, and a visual spectacular of the modern views that you will see on your travels. The Malta Experience is a great way to get an overall perspective and an excellent introduction to the sites on the islands.

AROUND VALLETTA

Valletta does not have a monopoly on history or wonderful architecture. Almost every settlement on the islands will have a building (often a church) that is worthy of note and exploration. The countryside is also littered with military remains. These include castles and lookout points from the time of the knights up until 19th and 20th century fortifications.

Floriana

Any trip to Valletta from around the island will entail traveling through Floriana, which sits just outside the gates of the capital. Floriana is named after military engineer Pietro Floriana, who was charged with the job of extending Valletta's defenses in the mid-16th century, and the bulwarks became a basis for the development of the town. It has wide streets and pretty squares putting one in mind of a Parisian *arrondissement*. Floriana was rebuilt after World War II, and her finest buildings faithfully recreated. You will find most of the foreign consulates and embassies here, along with Malta's police headquarters.

The arches pictured below are the Portes des Bombes, which serve as an entryway into Floriana.

The dome that dominates the skyline belongs to **St. Publius Church**, named after the Roman Governor who was converted to Christianity by St. Paul in A.D. 60. The square in front of the church has granary silos under the surface, which date from 1660. These were in continual use until the 1960s.

The arch marking the entrance to Floriana sits astride two lanes of a main road that bisects the town. Called the **Portes des Bombes**, it was erected in 1721 (left and right of it you can see the result of engineer Floriana's plan for new city walls) but has undergone several alterations since then, including a second arch that was inserted to allow passage of the now defunct Valletta to Mdina railway line.

Where Floriana meets Valletta you will find the bus terminal, always busy with people and vehicles. Next to this, against the Valletta city wall is **St. James' Ditch**, which hosts the huge Sunday morning market.

Rinella

Valetta sits at the western mouth of the Grand Harbor, and Point Rinella can be found at the eastern mouth, barely half a kilometer away as the crow flies, yet 20 minutes by car around the bay. On the point is Fort Ricasoli, with its beautiful gate dated 1698. It is now in a state of disrepair but is evidence that Malta has a difficult and expensive task ahead to preserve all of its very large historical sites.

Further east around the point is **Fort Rinella**. This 19th century fortification was built for only one purpose, to house the largest cannon ever built — a 100-ton cannon so massive that no other fortification could accommodate it. The muzzle-loaded gun required a team of 22 people to man it in action and it could penetrate 15.2 inches of metal at a distance of 8 km (7000 yds).

Next to the fort is the **Rinella Movie Park** (Mediterranean Film Studios — Malta). The film studios have been one of the success stories since independence, with a number of major movies filmed on Malta. This studio has the largest water tank facilities in Europe. You can tour the studios or enjoy the theme park, which has shows, theme sets and playgrounds.

> **Good morning – bongu (bonjoo)**

The "Three Cities" and the Cottonera Lines

Around Grand Harbor you will find Vittoriosa, Senglea and Conspicua, known collectively as "the three cities."

When the knights first arrived on Malta, they settled in **Vittoriosa** (then called Birgu, a name some Maltese still favor) — a narrow spit of land jutting out into Grand Harbor. They set about reinforcing older fortifications at the bayside point, which they renamed **Fort St. Angelo**. It was this fort that in 1565 withstood repeated Turkish attacks with 600 knights and fewer than 1,000 men-at-arms. Reinforced after the victory, the fort has remained unchanged in outline since 1689, though it was used as a naval station by the British (who renamed it H.M.S. St. Angelo). The Maltese government has leased part of the fort back to The Order of St. John, so much of the upper bastions are now off limits to the public.

The town of Vittoriosa sits behind the fort. Vittoriosa Square is diminutive but forms a central point for several thoroughfares through the town — the streets are still laid out as they were in Medieval times, with bends and curves rather than straight lines. Birgu developed according to the needs of the knights. Seven auberges and a hospital were built here, though these facilities were later transferred to Valletta. A convent built beside the hospital still has a community of sisters over 400 years later, and a bishop's palace built in 1542, which now serves as a school.

Vittoriosa's newly restored Naval Bakery lies alongside the waterfront, a perfect complement to the townscape.

Then, in 1574, another more powerful servant of the church arrived to oversee the deeds of the knights and the Maltese population. The Spanish Inquisition took up offices in what until then had been the old Law Courts. The institution was all-powerful until it was abolished by the French in 1798. Grand Inquisitors were charged with the responsibility of investigating any evidence of heresy. This they did with ruthless efficiency. They also acted as arbitrators in the case of disputes between the knights, Grand Master, and the Bishop. The plain façade of the **Inquisitors Palace** hides plain prison cells and dungeons on the lower floors, and highly decorated private apartments of the Inquisitors themselves above, including the Tribunal room where evidence was heard and verdicts were issued.

Down on the wharf side — which has been in use since ancient times — is a **church dedicated to St. Lawrence**. The original church dated 1530 has been adapted and embellished over the centuries, including the addition of a Baroque façade. The interior benefits from an altarpiece by Mattia Preti gracing one of nine altars. Outside the church, a small park surrounds the **Freedom Monument** with bronze figures depicting the departure of the last British serviceman who stepped onto a naval vessel from this wharf in 1979.

Enter the wharf under the arch at the waterside here. This area was a hive of activity under British rule because it was a major military outpost of the Empire. The British built a large Victualling Yard and bakery along the wharf edge of the inlet — named Dockyard Creek — to restock the ships and feed the garrison. Following their closure in 1979, the buildings were left to fall into decay but the Naval Bakery has been refurbished to house the **National Maritime Museum**. Here you

will find displays of salvage found in Maltese waters, along with naval uniforms and paintings. The naval tactic textbooks and models of ships on display were used in the training of naval cadets. There is also a section on traditional Maltese craft.

Vittoriosa was protected on the land side by a wall consisting of a series of bas-

Couvre Port is only the most impressive of Vittoriosa's defensible walls.

tions and curtains (sheer walls). Three gateways allowed entry and can still be seen. The most impressive is the **Couvre Port** dated 1727.

To the left of Vittoriosa is another spit of land on which you will find the city of **Senglea**, named after Grand Master Claude de la Sengle who built its fortifications in 1551. Safe Haven Garden at the very tip of the spit offers good views across the harbor to the Valletta skyline. It is protected by an ancient stone **vedette** atop a bastion, decorated by an eye and an ear indicating that it is all-seeing and all-hearing.

Today Senglea is a working city. Most of its population travels to the Malta Dry Docks at Frenchmen's Creek. The tradition of shipbuilding and repair carries on into modern times with huge cranes and jacks on the move every day.

Conspicua occupies a site at the head of Dockyard and Frenchmen Creeks abutting Senglea and Vittoriosa. It was the largest of the three cities in the 16th century but was badly damaged in World War II and was rebuilt as an industrial town.

All three "cities" were bound together in a huge fortification in the 1680s when the Grand Master Nicola Cottoner commissioned and paid for a massive outer protective wall in case of another attack. About 3 km (1.8 miles) of wall arced from the waters of Kalkara Creek (north of Vittoriosa) to Frenchmen's Creek. There were five entry gates, the cen-

The Magic Eye

All fishing boats in Maltese waters have an eye painted at each side of their bow. This is to allow the boat to see danger, and to ward off any evil spirits that may be out at sea. Every spring before the fishermen put their boats on the water for the summer, they will paint the eye afresh to give them maximum protection.

tral one of which has a bust of Cottoner and beautiful embellishments in stone. The new walls, which came to be known as the **Cottonera Lines**, can clearly be seen as you travel the area, and are as impressive now as they would have been to a Turkish janissary in the 17th century.

The Hypogeum and the Tarxien Temples

Paola and Tarxien are two busy towns, ten minutes by car journey from Valletta. Within their boundaries they have two very important ancient sites, both discovered in the early 19th century. The **Hal-Saflieni Hypogeum** (hypogeum is a Greek word meaning underground) began life as a simple cave where Neolithic settlers buried their dead. Sometime between 3800 and 2500 B.C., the population began to cut and shape the cave creating a second level of chambers, and later a third, until the caves reached downwards 12 m (40 ft) underground. The sheer scale of the hypogeum is astounding, and the workmanship involved is evidence of the sophistication of these ancient peoples. More then 700 human skeletons have been found here, and many artifacts excavated are now on display at the Archaeological Museum in Valletta.

The nearby **Tarxien Temples** (Tar-sheen) form a very important archeological record of life in the 4th millennium B.C. They were discovered in 1915, when a farmer, complaining about the huge stones that littered his fields and hindered his plowing, called someone to investigate the situation. Dr. Themistocles Zammit, a Maltese archeologist arrived and promptly excavated the whole site to discover three temples. There is no record of the farmer's reaction.

The Tarxien Temples show evidence of the great strides forward made by builders during the temple building phases. The middle temple here — dated at 3200 B.C. — is more substantial and accurate than earlier ones at Ġgantija on

Gozo. Libation holes, used to worship the gods of the underworld, can clearly be seen, but the many carved stone slabs depicting bulls and pigs are copies — the originals are at the Archeological Museum in Valletta.

The town of Tarxien itself is also interesting, for although the modern suburbs crowd the temple site, the heart of the old town is charming; its buildings changing little over the decades.

The Resorts

Lying to the left of Valletta is **Marsamxett Harbor**, (Marsam-shet) which is surrounded by several creeks

A visit to the Tarxien temples invariably brings out the archeologist in everybody.

and headlands. Nearest to Valetta is Sa Maison, where the regular ferry to Gozo has its base. The creek at **Msida** (M-sida) was once a major fishing port, but in recent years it has been transformed into a modern yacht marina. A few small *luzzu* (small fishing boats) still set sail from here, but sailboats and motor cruisers now line the jetties. **Manoel Island** juts out into the bay here. Fort Manoel watches over the comings and goings on the water and Phoenicia Glass has a workshop here, but the island is given over to numerous small boat repair yards — practical, but not necessarily beautiful.

The next five or six kilometers (3–4 miles) of coastline to the west have been a major focus for development in the last

Fishing boats line the waterfront by the church of St. Joseph dating back to 1892.

30 years. The small individual settlements of **Sliema**, **St. Julian's**, **St. George's**, and **Paceville** (pronounced *parch-a-*ville) now blend into one long strand of hotels, bars, cafés and nightclubs. St. Julian's has seen the most recent development with a rash of new five-star hotels, and the Portomaso Marina Complex. This area certainly has the most sophisticated entertainment and nightlife and it's where you'll find the young, affluent Maltese after dark.

THE SOUTHEAST COAST

The southeastern section of Malta is an interesting mixture of old and new, where tradition carries on beside 21st century industry. A number of bays offer shelter for boats, especially in the east. This is where you will find the fishing fleets

— and some of the best fish restaurants. **Marsascala** is the most easterly town on Malta. Its little fishing boats bob on the water of its narrow bay. Il-Kappana, a headland on the south side has been developed for tourism, with self-catering apartments, and some hotels.

> Enjoy an evening passeggiata or stroll, around the village square or along the promenade.

The St. Thomas Tower at the end of the headland is the most easterly building on Malta — work is in hand to refurbish the site.

South of Marsaskala is **Marsaxlokk** (marsa-shlok), with the largest fishing fleet in the Maltese islands. Tourist development has concentrated inland of the town, leaving the harbor area refreshingly unspoiled. Thousands of gaily painted *luzzu* sit on the water or rest on the dockside. You'll find the fisherman tending to the boats or mending nets, constantly chatting as they work. Informal fish restaurants have tables by the water where you can enjoy an alfresco lunch or dinner, and there is a daily market here with table linens and lace for sale.

Heading out towards the lighthouse and fort at Delimara Point, you will pass the Carmelite church of **Tas Silġ**, a site of religious worship for many centuries before the birth of Christ. Unfortunately, this area has been spoiled visually by a new power station, although the station has helped to bring reliable power supplies to the island.

Near the coastal town of **Birżebbuġa** is the fascinating cave system of Għar Dalam and a small museum displaying finds from the site. Għar Dalam cave runs 144 m (472 ft) into the limestone rock and its fissures link to caves in the west that were once an ancient watercourse. During the Pleistocene period this area was a haven for ancient hippopotamuses, elephant, and deer, whose remains were fossilized over millions of years. The bones of hundreds of specimens have been found here — indicating that Malta was once rich in water and vegetation. Notices in the caves indicate which layer of rock the bones were found in, and the museum displays thousands of bones in glass cases reminiscent of those found in a Victorian professor's study.

Birżebbuġa (Bear-jee-booga) has some tourist infrastructure, however, its best beach at Pretty Bay has been blighted by the building of a modern container port. Malta is the perfect central depot for container traffic in the Mediterranean and a container storage depot has been built on the site of an old British RAF station of Hal Far nearby.

An international airport, with one of Europe's longest runways, takes up a large amount of space in this southeastern area. Beyond the airport is a collection of villages

The yawning entrance to the Blue Grotto cave seems like a passageway into a magical world.

leading to several more natural attractions. **Żurrieq** is the largest of these villages, with the parish church of St. Catherine (1659) at its heart. Mattia Preti had a studio

Thank you–grazzi (graht-see)

and workshop here, and painted the altarpiece in the church.

Only a couple of minutes from **Żurrieq** are the cliff-tops above the Blue Grotto. Stop at the small gardens here to get a glimpse of the arched entrance to the grotto from above and watch the little boats enter and leave — it's a great photo opportunity! Drive down the steep road to the boat dock, set in a sheltered cove nearby (if you take the public bus you will have to walk down this road). The boats head out when full and take you on a 30-minute trip taking in **Blue Grotto** and several other smaller caves. Try to arrive before the sun gets too high in the sky because the reflections offer the most spectacular colors within the caves. These range from turquoise to mauve and they reflect to the cave ceilings for a visual spectacle. The Blue Grotto gets busy with tour groups at lunchtime, because refreshment can be found at the restaurants here.

A little way west of the grotto are the spectacular Neolithic remains of **Ħaġar Qim** and Mnajdra, on a hillside overlooking the tiny island of **Filfla** (once used by the British for bombing practice). The island is a bird sanctuary and is also home to a unique species of lizard. Ħaġar Qim, which sits atop the cliffs, was discovered as early as 1839 and consists of a series of temples in fan-like shape. Unfortunately it was constructed of soft stone and has weathered considerably. A number of "fat lady" statuettes were found here indicating its use as a fertility shrine, and there are even tethering loops for animals in the stone but no one is sure if these were used for sacrifice.

Mnajdra (M-naydra) sits below Ħaġar Qim, around 500 m from it. It is made up of two main temples dated at around

3400 B.C. and is probably the best-preserved on Malta. Its doorways are particularly fine, with posts and lintels. It is worthwhile climbing the slope behind the temples. From here you can get an overview of the whole structure and appreciate its size and complicated structure.

INLAND TO MDINA, RABAT, MOSTA, AND BEYOND

For many centuries until the arrival of the Order of St. John, the capital of Malta had been inland at Mdina. Today this small settlement displays many vestiges of its prestigious past and has numerous attractions to explore.

On the way is the small town of Attard. Just as you reach the main junction into town you will see the remains of the **Wignacourt Aqueduct**, commenced in 1610 to supply water to Valletta. Turn into Attard to find **St. Anton Palace and Gardens**, built in the late 1620s as a summer palace for Grande Master Antoine de Paule. He personally supervised the layout of the formal gardens that surrounded it. Subsequent Grand Masters added to the palace itself and the British added the veranda beneath the turret. Filled with paintings and fine art, the Palace is now the residence of the president of Malta. The gardens open to the public are beautifully kept — replete with flowers, especially in the spring — and decorated with fountains and statuary. A small enclosure has animals for petting. Various shows are held here throughout the year, with open-air concerts in the summer.

Past Attard, the main road leads to Mdina — you can see its walls and spires on the horizon. After a couple of minutes you will see a turning to the left, leading to Ta' Qali Craft Centre, near the National Sports Stadium. Ta' Qali has a number of artisans working in what was an old air base. You'll see lacemaking, glassblowing and potting, and you'll be able to buy straight from the manufacturer.

Finally, the walls of Mdina/Rabat loom large ahead. The Phoenicians called the town Maleth, and it was known in Roman times as Melita. In the 8th century, the Arabs transformed Mdina into a fortified citadel. They built impregnable walls around the site to protect it from enemy raids. Rabat (an Arab word which literally means suburb) grew outside its walls to service the city. **Mdina** was the center of power for several centuries — the *Università* met here — and has a wealth of fine architecture dating from Norman times. When the knights came and made their capital on the coast, Mdina

Two travelers walk through Mdina's main gate, and enter a remarkable medieval city.

was left as a backwater. The city was badly damaged in an earthquake in 1693 and it wasn't until the 1720s that work began to rebuild and include some open spaces for the population to enjoy. While the street plan remains essentially Medieval with several fine period palaces, many of public buildings date from the period of post-disaster Baroque building.

When you step through the main gate of Mdina past the majestic lion sculptures, you take a step back in time. No neon signs or fast-food joints (though local traffic is allowed), just a peace

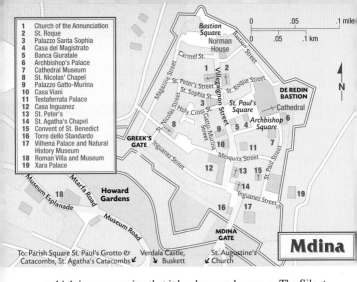

Mdina

Map Legend:

1. Church of the Annunciation
2. St. Roque
3. Palazzo Santa Sophia
4. Casa del Magistrato
5. Banca Giuratale
6. Archbishop's Palace
7. Cathedral Museum
8. St. Nicolas' Chapel
9. Palazzo Gatto-Murina
10. Casa Viani
11. Testaferrata Palace
12. Casa Inguanez
13. St. Peter's
14. St. Agatha's Chapel
15. Convent of St. Benedict
16. Torre dello Standardo
17. Vilhena Palace and Natural History Museum
18. Roman Villa and Museum
19. Xara Palace

To: Parish Square St. Paul's Grotto & Catacombs, St. Agatha's Catacombs ↙ Verdala Castle, Buskett ↓ St. Augustine's Church ↙

which is so pervasive that it has become known as The Silent City. You can spend time wandering along the narrow alleys and the city walls — it takes only a few minutes to stroll the 400-m (1300-ft) length of the main street. Just inside the main gate you will see the Magisterial Palace on your right. Built by Grand Master Manoel de Vilhena in the 1720s in French Baroque style, it was used as the seat of the commune — the local administrative assembly. The palace now houses the **Natural History Museum** with its collections of fossils, flora, fauna, and diagrams explaining the geological structure of the Maltese islands. Attached to the palace are buildings which once housed the law courts, and underneath these are the dungeons that were used to incarcerate and torture prisoners.

The **Mdina Dungeons** exhibit shows multifarious gory methods used to extract confessions, including the favored forms of torture used by each different ruling race. As you travel through the exhibit don't forget that these are the actual buildings where all of this took place, the small cells would really have held human prisoners. The scenes of disfigurement and amputation are rather realistic, especially in conjunction with the spine-chilling sound effects, and so it may not be suitable for young children.

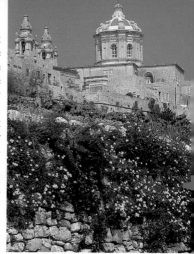

In the springtime, wild flowers grow around the Cathedral of St. Paul.

Many of the main attractions can be found on Villegaignon Street, which cuts through the heart of the town. As you turn onto Villegaignon Street, on your left is **Casa Inguanez**. This is the palace of the oldest noble family on Malta and its plain façade reveals its Norman heritage (1370). Several changes and renovations have been made over the centuries to what is essentially still a family home. Across the narrow street the **Chapel of St. Agatha** is dedicated to the Christian martyr who came to Malta to escape Roman persecution in the 3rd century. The church dates from 1471 and was re-designed in 1694.

You will find several costumed ladies offering fliers for attractions as you walk down the street here. In an area as small as Mdina there are four audio/visual walk-through attractions vying for your attention. On Villegaignon Street itself, in historic Palazzo Gatto Murina is **Tales of the Silent**

City, covering all aspects of Mdina's past. It also has a large gift shop and artisan area. Down the narrow alleyway of Mesquita Street you can find **The Mdina Experience**, and on the old Ramparts on Magazine Street is the newest attraction, **The Knights of Malta**, which concentrates on the

The Knights of St. John

The story of the Order of the Hospital of St. John of Jerusalem (the Knights Hospitallers) begins in the 11th century, when Italian merchants obtained permission from the Muslim caliph to set up a Christian hospice in Jerusalem. The calling of the order was principally to care for the sick, but in time the emphasis shifted to a military role, that of fighting for the faith. In 1187 the order were driven from Jerusalem by Saladin, and spent the following centuries fighting different Muslim leaders.

The knights took vows of poverty, chastity, and obedience. They were grouped in eight *langues*, or "tongues," three of them French (France being divided in the 13th century into France, Provence, and Auvergne). The other *langues* were Aragon, Castile, Italy, Germany, and England. (After the Reformation the English *langue* ceased to exist). Each *langue* built an *auberge* where they lived together.

Each langue was headed by a *pilier*, who had a set function: thus the *pilier* of Italy was Grand Admiral; the *pilier* of Provence was finance and ordnance manager; the *pilier* of France was head of the order's hospitals. Their head, the Grand Master, was elected for life and was subject only to the authority of the Pope.

As the years passed, the knights lapsed into careless and even dissolute ways. Corruption and internal dissension undermined the effectiveness and reputation of the order. Some of the original ideals of the Hospitallers are continued in the St. John Ambulance Association; the order itself, now based in Rome, does mainly charitable work.

Order, its history and its role on the island. All four are enter-taining, so much so that you may want to visit each one.

The main square in the citadel is flanked on the western side by the **Cathedral of St. Paul**, said to have been built on the site where St. Paul converted Publius, then the Roman Governor to Christianity, in A.D. 60. A church has existed on the site since the 4th century. This was enlarged under Count Roger's rule in 1090 and it was enlarged again in 1490. Following the earth-quake of 1693 it was completely redesigned, although some fea-tures such as the back arch of the church, and an Irish bogwood door dating from 900 do remain. The work was undertaken by Maltese architect Lorenzo Gafa' and is a masterpiece, with columns, twin bell towers and a fine dome. Inside you will find a marble font dating from 1495, and a beautiful pavement of marble tombstones commemorating religious dignitaries. The painting by Mattia Preti showing St. Paul riding on a white charger recalls the time during the Saracen attack of 1494 when it is said that St. Paul, mounted on a horse, appeared on the bat-tlements of Mdina to frighten the invaders away.

Across the small square outside the south door of the Cathedral is the Old Seminary. The main entrance of this majestic Baroque building — dating from 1729 — is flanked by two stone giants supporting an ornate stone bal-cony. Since 1968, the buildings have been used to house the **Cathedral Museum**, which has an impressive range of reli-gious artifacts and painting, including several medieval manuscripts and papal bulls relating to Malta. There is also an impressive numismatic collection including Maltese coins from Carthaginian times to the present day.

From the Cathedral, carry on along Villegaignon Street. You will be walking towards the corner statue of Madonna and Child on the left, which adorns the **Carmelite Church**. Riots against the French began here in 1798 when

Commandant Masson indicated that he was going to plunder the treasury of the church.

Opposite the church is the fourth audio/visual attraction — Medieval Times Adventure, and a little further along the street is **Palazzo Falzon** also known as "Norman House" a non-reconstructed look at life in Mdina in days gone by. The house is open to the public but only ten people at one time. Ring the bell at the arched entranceway and wait to be let in. Palazzo Falzon was begun in 1283 but, following the expulsion of the Jewish population from Malta in 1492, the synagogue that stood next to the house was disused and was bought by the Falzon family. The present house was built in 1495, utilizing the extra space. The stone walls and inner courtyard have changed little since that time and its proportions date back to medieval times. Paintings, furniture, and other everyday articles indicate a family life played out over the centuries and offers a fascinating glimpse behind Mdina's silent walls.

The interior of St. Paul's Grotto, a cave which has become a sort of shrine in devotion to St. Paul.

A little way beyond Norman House are the walls of the citadel at **Bastion Square**, offering views across nearby valleys towards Mosta. You can walk around the walls here, finding little nooks to explore. Make your way around to Magazines

> Excuse me –
> skuzi (skoo-zee)

Street where you will find **Greek Gate**, a less used entrance to the city but one much older than the main gate. Part of the bastion dates from Arab rule.

Beyond the walls of Mdina, **Rabat** could not be more of a contrast to the Silent City. It is a bustling town, which acted as the market place for Mdina, yet it too has historical treasures to reveal. Just outside Mdina's city wall the remains of a Roman house were discovered in 1881 on the site of a Muslim burial ground. In 1924 the site was covered by a mock Doric temple style building and designated the **Museum of Roman Antiquities**. The remains of the villa form the basement section and these comprise several mosaic floors, which are still in their original position. The more intricate details and centerpieces have been excavated and set on the wall allowing visitors to take a closer look at their exquisite detail. The tesserae are extremely small, allowing a great range of depth, shade, and movement in the finished mosaic. The scenes found at the house include one with nymphs punishing a satyr, which dates from the 1st century A.D. There are numerous marble statues and busts, including one of Claudius Tiberius Drusus (10 B.C.–A.D. 54) Roman Emperor from A.D. 41, and on the first floor are some beautiful artifacts recovered from the site and other Roman sites around Malta including a fine collection of glass and pottery.

From the Roman Villa take the main road to your right into the town. At the small but busy town square you will find the **Church of St. Paul** and the Chapel of St. Publius, underneath which is **St. Paul's Grotto** — a guide will be in the vicinity to

The great dome of Mosta church was built without the aid of a scaffolding.

unlock the gates for you. This small cave, hand cut out of the soft sandstone, is said to be the place where St. Paul and St. Luke spent their time after being shipwrecked on the island. Two small chambers can be viewed, the largest of which contains a statue of the apostle donated by Grand Master Pinto. Nearby are two small chapels dedicated to the Paul and Luke. Pope John Paul II visited the shrine in 1990.

Beyond this grotto within walking distance are several large grotto complexes, each of which were used for burials in early Christian times. **St. Paul's Catacombs** date from the 4th and 5th century and are the largest on Malta with several passages leading to multiple tomb recesses. The first main room at the bottom of the entrance stairs was used to conduct funeral services. **St. Agatha Catacombs** —— situated across the street —— are said to be the actual caves where the saint sought refuge against Roman oppression. These are decorated with fine religious frescoes dating from the 11th century.

Only 3 km (1.8 miles) northeast of Mdina is **Mosta**, a city whose major attraction can clearly be seen from the walls of the old capital. The massive **Rotunda** of the church of St. Mary has the third largest dome in Europe and is a masterpiece of design and building skills completed without the aid of interior scaffolding. The church was designed by George Grognet de Vasse, a Maltese engineer of French origin, and is based on the Pantheon in Rome. Its dome is 51 m (167 ft) high and 45 m (147 ft) in diameter with walls 6 m (19 ft) thick.

In a famous incident during World War II, a German bomb fell on to the Rotunda, piercing the dome and falling into the

> **Don't call the people of Gozo Maltese; they are proud to be Gozitans.**

church below. It did not explode, attributed by worshippers to the intervention of their patron — the Virgin Mary. You will see a replica of the bomb on display in the sacristy.

Mosta has grown dramatically in recent years as the fame of its Rotunda has grown, but the center of the town still displays its Medieval past and it is worthwhile taking time to explore the narrow alleys and streets.

To the south west of Mosta and Mdina, Malta becomes more rural, with only a few farming settlements surrounded by acres of terraced fields. The roads here are narrow and a little bumpy, but your journey will be rewarded with scenes of rural life. You will see vestiges of old fortifications, including a defensive wall running across the center of the island, originally built by the British during the Victorian period. **The Victoria Lines** as they are known, became something of a white elephant as warfare changed in the 20th century. Onwards towards the village of Mġarr are more Neolithic remains at **Ta' Ħaġrat** and **Skorba**, however these are not generally open to the public. Inquire with the tourist office if you would like to tour them.

Beyond Rabat to the south, the main road leads down towards the coast. **Verdala Palace** and *Buschetto* or **Buskett Gardens** are on the right off this road. The Palace was originally a hunting lodge for Grand Master de Verdale. The modest property, which he built in 1595, was enlarged and improved by subsequent Grand Masters over the years to the graceful three stories of today. Verdala Palace is the summer residence of the president and the house is not open to the public. The extensive gardens are now split into two sections, those which form the private gardens of the palace, and an area of natural woodland beyond which is a favorite picnic site for Maltese families on summer weekends. A large horticultural show is held here on 29 June of each year.

South of Buskett are the curious remains called "**Clapham Junction**" after a complicated railway junction system in England. These are some of the best examples of the Neolithic grooves in the limestone rock thought to have been made by the temple builders. The theory argues that these ancient peoples quarried rock from nearby sites and dragged the large megaliths on primitive carts to their religious sites. Over time their regular routes were marked by deep tracks. No one has yet proved this theory correct, but in any case, Clapham Junction is lined with several sets of deep ruts.

The road from Rabat stops abruptly at **Dingli Cliffs**, named after a nearby village. The precipitous drops along much of the south coast are awe-inspiring and are at their most spectacular around Dingli. There are several walking trails in the area, east to the pretty secluded cove of **Ghar Lapsi,** or west to the highest point on Malta at 250 m (820 ft) above sea level, marked by the **Madliena Chapel**.

When the Bells Fall Silent

You will become used to hearing the sound of the church bells that are rung regularly to call the faithful to prayer, but the bells fall silent during Easter. It is a tradition for the bells not to toll from the evening of Maundy Thursday until the evening of Easter Sunday. At this time an instrument called a *coqlajta* is used to call the people to church. The coqlajta is wooden instrument, a hollow cross set in a wooden jig. As the cross is turned, the shafts strike wooden pegs, making a distinctive hollow sound. It is unique in the Christian world.

THE NORTHWEST

The northwest of Malta has traditionally been less populated than the southeast. In this region you'll find much more farming activity, and much more open space. The northern coast has two resorts with lots of accommodation for tourists, with a different character than the Sliema/St. Julian's area. One main road travels the northern coastline leading to the small ferry port of Ċirkewwa at Malta's western tip.

Many visitors have a soft spot for the cartoonish charm of Popeye's village film set.

Once you leave the resort areas behind, you'll have a clear view of the limestone coastline and azure water. Pleasure craft speed along, passing stationary fishing boats. Fishermen also sit at the water's edge keeping a lonely vigil for the night's supper. Sentinel stone towers dot the coastline, once part of an important communication network ready to warn of invasion.

At **Baħar iċ-Cag-ħaq** you will find two attractions to thrill the children. A water park with slides, pools and fair rides is open during the summer months (April–Oct), and next door to it is **Mediterraneo Marine Park**, a must for lovers of marine mammals. The park has fun-loving sea lions and playful dolphins that perform twice daily in the summer months. You can also watch pelicans waddle along at feeding time. The Marine Park also operates education programs, which involve getting behind the scenes with the animal trainers and caregivers who keep the animals healthy and happy. These are open to the public and last for 90 minutes.

The road carries on around the coast to **Salina Bay**, named for the salt flats which have been used for centuries to produce this most important of minerals. Salina Bay marks the start of the second major area developed for tourists, which stretches around the headland of Qawra. This area is characterized by more self-catering accommodations and fewer large hotels than Sliema/St. Julian's. The nightlife is a little more raucous and a little less sophisticated. Having said that, there are enough bars, clubs and eateries to satisfy the thousands of people who enjoy coming here every year.

As you travel around the headland **Qawra** melds into **Buġibba** (Boo-jee-ba), a modern town whose only link with history seems to be **Wignacourt Tower** — sitting amongst the modern buildings overlooking the waters of **St. Paul's Bay**. This is said to be the place where the apostle landed following his dramatic shipwreck. Just inland from Buġibba, in the small town of **Burmarrad**, is the simple church of **San Pawl Milqghi** (St. Paul Welcomed), said to be the site where he first made contact with the Maltese people. The bay of St Paul's has two islands lying offshore. One of these has a large statue of the apostle.

At the head of the bay you'll see signs leading to the opposite coast, to Golden Bay and it's neighboring Ghajn Tuffieha Bay. The road passes fertile land and numerous small farms. Both bays are sandy but **Ghajn Tuffieha** (ayn-tuffia) is part of a reserve and therefore has not been developed. The cliffs around it out to the headland are accessible by footpath and are popular with hikers. **Golden Bay** has refreshment kiosks, a large hotel, and a car park just behind the beach. The sand is great for castle building and the water has no undertow, making it safe for children.

Mellieħa bay is home to a fishing harbor as well as a splendid beach, distinguished by its yellow sun parasols.

Continuing along the main road around St. Paul's Bay you will begin to climb up away from the coast. The road cuts across the verdant **Mistra Valley**, through a fragrant pine copse. At the top of the hill there is a turning to the village of **Selmun** with its Knights Palace on the hill, now a hotel with large modern extension. Mellieħa village at the crest of the hill was once a remote settlement (built on the hill for protection against raiders from the sea). Over the ridge, you start to drop again and you can see the wide sandy beach of Mellieħa Bay below. Just before you reach the bay you will find a turn to the left, leading you to **Anchor Bay**, a beautiful natural cove, great for diving and swimming. Here you will also find

Village, originally built in 1980 as a set for the film *Popeye* starring Robin Williams. Popeye Village is a series of "kooky" buildings that formed Popeye and Olive Oyl's hometown,

Sweethaven, in the film. It was built of Canadian lumber on wooden stakes imported from Holland. It's a fun place for kids to explore — but better if you have actually seen the film.

Mellieħa Bay is arguably the best beach on Malta and it is often very busy in the summer. There are lots of facilities here if you want to stay for the day, or you could bring a picnic. Behind the beach is a grassy, marshy area, which is an important haven for breeding birds, both native and migratory. The marsh is a protected environment called **Ghadira Nature Reserve** (*ghadira* means lake), which is open to the public in the mornings when it is not breeding season.

> **Greet people when passing in the street.**

From Mellieħa Bay it's only a short ride up and over **Marfa Ridge** to Ċirkewwa and the short ferry crossing to Gozo (the ferry from Sa Maison near Valletta takes one hour; this crossing takes only 30 minutes). At the top of Marfa Ridge there are junctions with secondary roads that lead both left and right along the ridge. Both offer excellent panoramic views of Malta and across to Comino and Gozo. On your left you'll see the **Red Tower** 50 m (164 ft) from the main road, constructed in 1647 and now in the process of being refurbished; it acted as a communications post with the knight's garrison on Gozo.

Views across the Comino Channel are beautiful, with the domes of the churches of Gozo clearly visible on the skyline across the straits. There's very little tourist infrastructure on this side of Malta, and for this reason it is many peoples' favorite part of the island. Maltese families have small chalets by the sea where they come to enjoy summer weekends.

GOZO AND COMINO

The nearest most people get to tiny Comino (2.7 sq. km in total) is gazing at it from the deck of the ferry ships traveling to Gozo. There is only a small permanent population on the island, no vehicles, and one hotel open in summer only. For this reason Comino is a great place to get away from it all — for walking and relaxing. The most famous attraction of the island is a magnet for divers and boaters. The **Blue Lagoon** is a shallow harbor area with a sandy bottom. The light reflected through the water gives it a brilliant azure color (you can catch a fleeting glimpse of it from the ferry), reminiscent of the Caribbean. You can take a boat trip from Valletta or many resorts on the northern coast of Malta.

Gozo is Malta's smaller sibling, and at 67 sq km, is less than a quarter of the size. Its history mirrors that of its neighbor yet it has a different character than Malta. Life moves more slowly here and seems less affected. There are far fewer visitors (there are less than 10 major hotels here), and much more land is given over to agriculture. It has more hills

The town of Mġarr slopes down into a harbor, which contains various moored ferries and fishing vessels.

than Malta, and is much greener due to more rainfall. Gozo still retains much more of its traditional lifestyle and this is what makes the island such a pleasure to visit. Gozo is great for cycling and hiking. It also has some of the best diving in the Mediterranean.

One thing you will immediately notice is the lack of concrete buildings. Of course Gozo isn't immune to development

> **Good evening/night–
> bonswa (bonswah)**

but most new buildings are constructed of sandstone (the same stone used in the numerous forts and castles), which weathers beautifully and looks wonderful in the mellowing sunlight. Many Gozitans (as the people of Gozo are called) emigrated in the years after World War II and some are now returning to enjoy their old age in the place of their birth. You'll see houses with names such as "Waltzing Matilda" or "Stars and Stripes," a sure sign of fond memories of adopted countries far away.

Unless you take the helicopter service, which lands at a spot on top of the hill, your first real view of Gozo will be the port of **Mġarr** (M-ghar) whose buildings extend down a hillside and around a small cove. The commercial ferry port is functional rather than pretty — it's always busy because this is where you buy your ferry tickets (whereas on the Malta side you simply drive right onto the ferry). You'll find a tourist information office and a bank here, along with a couple of cafés. Beyond the ferry port is a delightful fishing harbor that doubles as a yacht harbor in the season.

The empty gunning placements of **Fort Chambray** look down from the cliff-tops, over the approaches. The fort was built in 1749 with the personal funds of Jacques-Francois de Chambray who was Commander of the fleet of the Order of St. John. On the opposing side of the harbor Our Lady of Lourdes Church protects the souls of the population. You'll have to climb up and out of the harbor to make it anywhere on Gozo. For cyclists this is an early challenge.

There are several settlements on the island but most roads to these lead from the capital, Victoria, like the spokes on a wheel. On the way to the capital the road passes through the village of Għajnsielem where you will find the **Gozo Heritage** attraction. Here, through a series of specially-lit tableau and a special soundtrack, you can journey through the history of the island.

Nearby at **Xewkija** (Shew-kiya) you'll find a beautiful church. Its dome, which can be viewed quite easily from the main road, rivals Mosta in size. Local people made the building of the church, dedicated to St. John the Baptist, possible with their donations. Though commenced in 1951, it was more than 25 years before it was consecrated. You'll find a life-size replica of the old parish church inside the Rotunda.

Victoria lies at the heart of the island and it is the administrative, business, and social hub of Gozo. The town has only been called Victoria since 1897, when it was renamed by the British in honor of Queen Victoria's silver jubilee. You'll find that local Gozitans will refer to it as Rabat, its original Arab name.

The city is made up of two parishes: St. George and St. Mary's. There is a keen ri-

This church, dedicated to St. John the Baptist, can be seen throughout the valley.

valry between the two as they vie to throw the best *festas* with the loudest and most spectacular fireworks. The main thoroughfare through town, Republic Street, leads to **It-Tokk Square** (now officially known as Independence Square) with its cafés and daily morning market. At the west end of the square is the Tourist Information Office housed in a circular building dating from 1733, which was the **Banco Guiratale**. The old town, to the south and west of It-Tokk, is a maze of narrow alleys where you can find ladies making lace in the shade of their doorways. There are also numerous craft and antique shops, with a special quarter for old metal kitchenware and other collectibles. Walk from It-Tokk just one block south to the St. George's Square where you will find the **Basilica of St. George**. Built between 1672 and 1678 — though it was badly damaged in the earthquake in 1693 — it is richly decorated, with ceilings painted by Italian artist Giovanni Battista Conti. The ornate statue of the patron saint is made of wood carved in 1841. This is carried through the streets on the festival day (3rd Sunday in July). A painting by Mattia Preti over the choir altar depicts the knight poised at the moment of his victory over the dragon.

Walk up the street opposite the Tourist Office to reach the Citadel. On the way you'll pass the **Gozo 360°** attraction at the Citadel Theater/Cinema. This 25-minute long film takes you on a visually spectacular journey around the island, and it includes a multilingual musical accompaniment.

The Citadel at Victoria is much smaller than Mdina but was created at the same time, in the 8th century when Arab rulers built the imposing defensive walls. The whole settlement suffered badly during Ottoman raids in 1551 and in the earthquake of 1693. Although the church and several administrative buildings were rebuilt, much of the citadel still lies in ruins. The tiny community has a peaceful yet profound

*The ruins of Rabat's Citadel gives us a reminder of the
battles undertaken for the conquest of these islands.*

atmosphere, especially if you find it empty (try early in the
morning or after sunset). The most imposing building is **St.
Mary's Cathedral,** erected soon after the earthquake and
designed by Gafa, who also designed St. Paul's in Mdina.
Unfortunately there was not enough money available to fin-
ish the cathedral and a proposed dome was never erected.
Later, in 1732, the Italian artist Antonio Manuele was con-
tracted to paint a marvellous *trompe l'oeil* on the ceiling of
the church creating the effect of a dome. **The Cathedral
Museum** is accessed through a door at the side of the building. Here you'll find gold and silver items that comprise the
Cathedral treasury, along with vestments, prayer books, and
other items. St. Mary's observed day is the Feast of the
Assumption on 15 August, when the statue of Our Lady is
carried through the crowded streets.

The square in front of the Cathedral is flanked by two important administrative buildings. On the left is **Chapter's**

Hall, the old ecclesiastical court. This was first erected in 1496 but has made several architectural transitions. On the right, the **Courts of Justice** were once the Governor's Palace. Look for the escutcheon of Grand Master Wignacourt on the façade; he was head of the order when this building opened at the beginning of the 18th century.

The arch to your left leads to Bondi's Palace, once the meeting place of the Gozo commune or council. The building dates from the 16th century and now houses **Gozo Archaeological Museum**. The museum has an excellent collection of artifacts from many eras of the islands' history, including a number of effigies depicting both fleshy female figures and emaciated forms found at the Neolithic sites. Nearby is a craft area, and you can climb on to the bastions from stone stairs to the right of the museum. To the left you can see the original main gate to the citadel.

In the last decade a number of old Norman houses in the

citadel have been restored at the start of an ongoing process to rebuild the interior. The finest is the **Folklore Museum** on Milite Bernardo Street right of the Cathedral. The exhibits explain the traditional lifestyle of Gozitans with original farm machinery, weaving looms, and lace-making paraphernalia. The building itself is

The Azure Window rock formation pictured here is a timeless visual treat.

also fascinating with stones staircases, narrow corridors and cool stone walls. Look out also for the **Natural Sciences Museum** with its collection of rocks and fossils. There are also old armaments displayed in the old citadel granary.

The countryside of Gozo offers many attractions, and acres of natural beauty. West of Victoria is the traditional farming settlement **Gharb** (the name means west in Arabic and is pronounced Arb) but before you reach the village, turn off left towards the village of **San Lawrenz**. At this junction is the workshop of **Gozo Glass**, on the left. The craftsmen work every day, so you can watch pieces being blown, as pigment is added to produce their characteristic vivid hues. The parish church at San Lawrenz sports dome is painted a warm red color reminiscent of Italian and Greek settlements. The main road through the village leads on towards the coastline. Just beyond the village on the left is **Ta' Dbeigi Craft Village** where you can see lace being made or pottery being painted. Your final destination is Dwejra Point on the west coast, where there are three remarkable natural attractions.

Just off the coast of Dwejra Bay is **Fungus Rock**, much prized by the Knights for the curative plants found on its surface — they built a tower here in 1651, to watch the bay and protect the plants. Today the rock is off-limits to the public.

North of Fungus Rock is perhaps the most spectacular of the three attractions here. In a rocky outcrop, an arch of rock several hundred feet high has been eroded by the power of wind and waves. Looking through the arch reveals a landscape of sea and sky, giving it the epithet **Azure Window**. As you walk across the rocks to take a close view of the window, look down at your feet. The sedimentary sandstone here has hundreds of fossilized sand dollars embedded in it, brought to the surface by gradual erosion.

The area around Marsalforn, with its fishing harbor and sea wall, seems perfectly tailored for an enjoyable stroll.

Set back from the sea is a small saltwater lake where pretty painted boats await their passengers. This is the **Inland Sea**, linked by a natural tunnel through the rocks to the Mediterranean Sea beyond. It has been used for centuries as a safe haven for boats in winter. The passenger boats travel through the tunnel emerging to explore the coastline at the other side of the Azure Window — a journey that takes about 20 minutes.

Traveling back along the main road to Victoria you will see a turning to **Ta' Pinu** on your left. This spectacular church is, like St. John's at Xewkija, a relatively young building consecrated in 1931, but it was built on the site of a much older chapel from the 16th century. Ta' Pinu has a fascinating story. In 1883 Carmela Grima a local woman came to the old chapel to pray. She heard a voice yet she was alone in the building. Gradually she realized that the voice was coming from the altarpiece — a painting depicting the Virgin Mary. Following this, several people who came to pray here claimed miracle cures, and gradually the church became a shrine. In 1920 the work started on this larger church to accommodate the increasing number of pilgrims who were visiting Ta' Pinu. In 1990 Pope John Paul II held a mass on the large esplanade outside the church. Beyond Ta' Pinu across the valley you'll see the lighthouse at **Gordan**, set on a mound offering fine views of the west of the island.

On the coast north from Victoria is **Marsalforn**, the most developed resort on the island. The collection of small hotels, bars and discotheques around the narrow bay is lively in summer, although not to the extent of the resorts on Malta. There is a promenade around the bay where local families will come to stroll in the sea air, escaping the heat of their inland village streets.

South of Victoria, the coast has only one settlement. The beautiful site of **Xlendi** (Shlen-dee) set in a narrow *wied* or valley, with a sheltered harbor and fleet of small fishing boats bobbing on the calm water. The tiny community has swelled in recent years and modern sandstone apartment blocks now fill the valley, but this does not yet spoil Xlendi's beauty. There are several fine restaurants here, making it a favorite place for lunch. You can then sit and admire the view or take to the hills along the footpaths radiating out along the cliff sides.

Further east along the cliffs is **Ta' Ċenċ** (Ta-chench) that has a five star hotel and numerous fine houses. The land here has ancient dolmen, burial mound and cart ruts to explore. There's a pretty footpath down to the cove at **Mġarr Ix-Xini** (M-ghar ish-ini) with fantastic views over the knight's tower surrounded by typical Gozitan landscape. This is a good excursion on foot but there are no facilities at Ix-Xini, so take a picnic or at least a drink and a snack.

North east of Victoria is the sizeable settlement of **Xagħra** (Sha-grah), set on one of the typical hills which dot the Gozitan landscape. There are good views of the surrounding area, which may be one of the reasons why it was chosen as the site of a temple during Neolithic times. On the southern flank of modern Xagħra is the **Temple of Ġgantija** (Jig-antiya) the oldest free-standing structure yet discovered in the world.

Ġgantija means giant, and the huge stones of these two temples are said to have been set in place around 3500 B.C. They were excavated in the 1820s, and a range of statuary and pottery was discovered which is now displayed in the archeology museums in Victoria and Valletta. The structure was revealed to be an inner wall of limestone and an outer wall of coralline — a harder rock. Each unit has two pairs of apses. In the inner apse they have a niche with stone altar.

A lone beach parasol and shrine give some character to the beach at Ramla Bay, the only wide sandy beach on Gozo.

The two temples have a common forecourt where it is thought the congregation would have gathered for worship.

Xagħra has other attractions to offer. It sits atop a porous limestone ridge and the whole area is cut with caves and ancient underground watercourses, and two are open to the public. Both **Ninu's Cave** and **Xerri's Cave** offer huge stalactites and stalagmites and both lie under family homes. You'll have a family member as a guide to take you down narrow steps into the caves beneath.

> **Relax–punctuality is not too important around the islands**

Beyond Xagħra, on the north east coast is **Ramla Bay**, the only wide sandy beach on Gozo — in fact *ramla* means sandy in Maltese. Not surprisingly, it can become busy though — if you can't find a spot on the sand, you can explore the remains of a small Roman structure just off the beach, and there are footpaths in the hills around. One path leads to Calypso's Cave, said to be the site in Homer's *Odyssey* where Ulysses was held captive by a nymph. The walk from Ramla Bay is easy and the views impressive, but you may find the fabled cave disappointing.

East of Ramla Bay there are some beautiful coves. Both **San Blas Bay** and **Daħlet Qorrot** take a little effort to reach but reward those who do with unspoiled beauty and peace and quiet.

The high ground in this part of Gozo is topped by the fast growing settlement of **Nadur** known for its Carnival parade, where local people dress in grotesque masks and generally make mischief — a kind of adult "trick or treat." Many of the newer houses here have been built for ex-patriots from countries around the world. They spare no expense in creating the most beautiful façades; the ornate sandstone balconies and columns are a fitting continuation of traditional Gozitan building techniques.

Malta Highlights

All state owned museums have the following opening hours, which are liable to change at short notice. Call the Malta Tourism Authority Infoline on 9973 0000 if in doubt.

Malta

1 Oct–15 June: Mon–Sat 8:15am–5pm; Sun 8:15am–4pm. 16 June–30 Sept: Daily 7:45am–2pm. Closed public holidays.

Gozo

Mon–Sat: 1 Oct–31 March Mon–Sat 8:30am–4:30pm; 1 April–30 Sept 8:45am–4:30pm; Sun 8.30am–3pm. Closed public holidays.

Fort St. Elmo Valletta. No phone. 16th-century fort. Open Sat 1pm–5pm, Sun 9am–5pm. Admission fee. (see page 35)

Grand Harbor Tour. From Sliema marina; Tel. 2134 3373. The best way to take in the amazing size of the Grand Harbor and her fortifications. Admission fee. (see page 85)

Grand Master's Palace. Valletta; Tel. 2122 1221. Knights of St. John Grand Master's palace and office. 16th–18th century armory and palace rooms on view. Open state hours. Admission fee. (see page 32)

National War Museum. Fort St. Elmo, Valletta; Tel. 2122 2430. Photographs and artifacts relating Malta's role in WWII. Open state hours. Admission fee. (see page 35)

The Malta Experience. Valletta; Tel. 2124 3776. Audio-visual journey of the history and landscape of the islands. Hourly tours Mon–Fri 11am–4pm; Sat, Sun 11am–1pm. (see page 39)

Upper Barracca Gardens. Valletta. This small park offers superb views across the Grand Harbor towards Vittoriosa and Senglea. Free. (see page 38)

St. John's Co-Cathedral. Valletta; Tel. 2122 0536. Huge church with magnificent decoration. Open Mon–Fri 9:30am–1pm; 3:30pm–4:30pm; Sat 9:30am–1pm. (see page 30)

The Inquisitors Palace. Vittoriosa; Tel. 2182 7006. Headquarters of the Spanish Inquisition on Malta. Open state hours. Admission fee. (see page 43)

Mdina. Medieval Citadel. Free (see page 53)

Cathedral of St. Paul, Villegaignon Street, Mdina; Tel. 2145 4136. 18th-century church. Open Mon–Sat 9am–1pm, 2pm–4:30pm. Free. (see page 57)

Hal-Saflieni Hypogeum, Burials Street, Paola. Prehistoric underground temple and burial chamber. Entry by pre-booked ticket only; tel: 2123 7747. (see page 46)

Blue Grotto. Caves cut into the limestone cliffs where the water is a bright azure blue. Open daily in daylight hours, weather permitting. Admission fee (boat hire). (see page 51)

The Rotunda, Mosta; Tel. 2143 3826. Third-largest free-standing dome in Europe. Open daily 9am–noon, 3pm–5pm and for services after 5pm. Free. (see page 60)

Ghar Dalam, Birzebbuga. Cave system where remains of fossilized hippopotamus and elephants were discovered. Open State hours. Admission fee. (see page 49)

Hagar Qim/Mnadjra. No phone. Neolithic temple structures. Open state hours. Admission fee. (see page 51)

Marsaxlokk. Fishing village with harbor full of small colorful *luzzu* fishing boats. (see page 49)

Tarxien Temples. Neolithic Temples Street, Tarxien; Tel. 2182 5579. Neolithic temple complex. Open state hours. Admission fee. (see page 46)

Gozo

The Azure Window. Natural arch eroded in the rock. Daylight hours. Free. (see page 73)

The Citadel. Fortified settlement with walls from the first millennium and houses from the 15th century. Free. (see page 70)

The Archeological Museum. Tel. 2155 6144. 15th-century palace with artifacts from Gozo's ancient past. Open state hours. Admission fee. (see page 29)

Ggantija Temple. Tel. 2155 3194. Megalithic temple; the oldest standing structure in the world. Open state hours. Admission fee. (see page 76)

Xlendi. A tiny inlet with bobbing fishing boats and great restaurants. Free. (see page 75)

WHAT TO DO

SHOPPING

Lying at a crossroads in the Mediterranean, Malta has always been a trading island and merchants have always played an important part in its economy. You'll find that the friendly shopkeepers are eager to invite you into their stores to show you their wares, but are not so persistent that you'll find it a hassle.

Over the centuries, a number of traditional handicrafts developed which now form the basis of the typical souvenirs that you'll want to bring home with you.

Where to Shop

Malta is a great place for browsers. There are no major malls and only a couple of smaller shopping arcades in the modern resort area of Sliema. In contrast, the narrow streets of Valletta, Mdina/Rabat and Victoria have a wealth of smaller shops hidden away around every corner. Their wares spill out into the streets enticing you to take a look.

Markets are also very popular and there is a regular timetable for every town. The major markets in Valletta are the flea market on Merchants Street, and the huge Sunday market at St. James' Ditch. Most markets sell everything from fresh fruit and vegetables to collectibles, even animals — for pets or for cooking! Many of the market stallholders who sell tourist souvenirs will be able to take payment by credit cards. It may pay to research beforehand the quality and price of a particular item before you buy. Markets take place in the mornings; often the stallholders will have packed away by noon.

There are also two craft centers for you to explore. Here you can not only buy goods, but also see the craftsmen in action. Ta' Qali on Malta is situated near Mdina, and on Gozo you will find the craft centre at Ta' Dbiegi, San Lawrenz, on the road to the Azure Window.

If you are just looking for knick-knacks or T-shirts, you'll find shops in abundance all across the islands.

What to buy

Lace: Only a few years ago it was common to see the women of every village sitting out in their shady courtyards making lace. Today, this remarkable handicraft is becoming rare — with few young women interested in learning the skill and cheap machine-produced lace flooding the market. On Gozo you will have more success at finding ladies working on lace, but you will be able to buy items on Malta.

Out of all the islands, Gozo has the largest concentration of women who still practice the fine art of lacemaking.

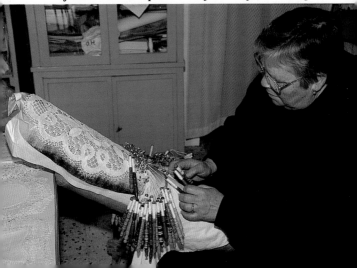

Pictured here is a sampling of the unique style of glass-ware that emanates daily from the Gozo Glass Studio.

Prices for fine hand-produced lace are reasonable and the workmanship is superb. You can buy items as small as a handkerchief or as large as bed linen or table linen, and in a variety of colors and patterns.

Knitted, woven, and crocheted goods are also abundant, and offer good value for money. Most ladies will sit out on summer evenings with knitting needles or crochet hooks working on items. Sweaters are popular — very useful on those cooler spring or fall evenings — and come in sizes to fit from the smallest baby to the largest man. Woven rugs are another practical item for the floor or as a bed throw. Made of wool or cotton, they are machine washable, easy to pack, and you will find numerous examples in Maltese family homes.

Maltese artisans have been creating items from silver for generations. You can find items such as picture frames, spoons, and christening mugs, but by far the most common items are those made out of silver fil-igree — items fashioned from fine silver wire. You will be able to watch

> How much? Kemm (pronounced kehm)

people at work in various retail workshops around the islands. Larger pieces you can buy include small bon-bon dishes or sculptures — galleons or animals feature prominently — or smaller items such as jewelry. The Maltese cross is of course very popular, as a brooch or on a chain, and appropriate as a remembrance of your time here. Gold is also very popular, as can be seen in the shops on St Lucia Street in Valletta.

Glass: It is handmade on both Malta and Gozo. The distinctive bright colors that swirl within each piece are introduced by adding powdered pigments as the glass is in its molten state. A range of items is produced, from vases to bowls to perfume bottles. Each item is produced in colors reflecting the dominant hues of the islands; the blues and aquas of the sea, verdant greens of the spring landscape, and the beiges of the sand and rocks in the hot summer sun. Mdina Glass can be found at the Ta' Qali Craft Centre. On Gozo, Gozo Glass has its studio at San Lawrenz on the main road of the village.

Pottery: It has been produced here since Malta's earliest history — witness the amazing artifacts in the archaeological museums of each island which date from thousands of years B.C., from Megalithic statuary to Roman amphora. Modern potters use both traditional and modern designs and you can buy pieces with a range of glazes.

Edibles: One theory about the origin of Malta's name is that it came from *melita*, the Greek word for honey. It indicates how important this foodstuff was to the islands in ancient times. Today honey is used to sweeten a range of Maltese dishes and you can buy pots of it to take home.

Cheese is one of the major products, particularly on Gozo, where it is still hand produced on small farms. The small rounds of sheep's milk cheese can be compared with Italian mozzarella and are served fresh, covered in herbs or pepper, or preserved in olive oil with sun-dried tomatoes.

For those with a sweet tooth, the nougat and toffee produced here is excellent. You can buy large blocks of both at stalls in every market and at *festas*.

Malta also produces an unusual alcoholic liqueur. Bajtra is made from the juice of the prickly pear — found in abundance all across the islands — which imparts a purple hue to the liquid. The juice is flavored with herbs and honey, and the resulting drink is unique. Bajtra is said to have been the favorite "tipple" of the Knights during their final years of decline and dissolution.

Antique shops abound in Rabat, offering anyone the right to take a piece of the Maltese islands home with them.

ENTERTAINMENT

Day Cruises: Take a tour of the Grand Harbor or a day cruise around the island with time for swimming and snorkelling. You can depart on a state-of-the-art catamaran, miniature cruise ship, a Turkish *gulet*, or a gaff-rigged schooner (pretend that you're a pirate). Captain Morgan offers the most comprehensive service, with several sizes of craft. They can even offer an underwater safari boat with Perspex keel, which allows you to enjoy the underwater environment without getting wet. Contact them at Dolphin Court, Tigné Seafront, Sliema; Tel. 2134 3373; fax 2133 2004; website <www.captainmorgan.com.mt>.

Aerial Tours: Take to the air to get a birds eye view of the islands. This is especially worthwhile to look at Grand Harbor, Mdina, and Victoria, as well as the beautiful coastline and azure waters. Both helicopters and light aircraft offer pleasure flights lasting anywhere from 20 minutes to one hour. Contact Captain Morgan Cruises for details of the helicopter service. Leisure Flight Services can provide the service in a light aircraft Barton Broad House, Triq Freemantle, Naxxar; Tel. 2148 3821.

Land Cruises: Take a four-wheel drive safari to the most remote points on the islands. You'll see vestiges of the Malta of the past and see just how diverse these tiny islands are. Captain Morgan Cruises offers jeep safaris with an experienced leader. Drivers must be over 25. Gozo Explorer offer tailor-made Jeep tours of the island, catering for specific interests or just general sightseeing. They can be contacted at 26 Comino Street, Għajnsielem, Gozo; Tel. 2156 1010; e-mail <maltesefalcon@orbit.net.mt>.

NIGHTLIFE

Malta has quite a sophisticated range of nightlife for such a small island. This centers on the resort areas of St. Julian's,

"The Knights of St. John Experience," a walk-through exhibition, is perfect for those in a medieval state of mind.

Sliema, and Buġibba where the large hotels and self-catering apartment blocks have been built. There are numerous bars and English-style pubs, along with an increasing number of wine bars. Many of these have live music or, at the very least, are equipped with superior sound systems. Later in the evening you can head out to a club — Matrix in Paceville, St. George's is the most popular at the moment — but be prepared to take your place in line at many establishments because the local Maltese jet-set also head out, particularly on weekends.

Most large hotels will also have a schedule of entertainment, from dinner-dances to folklore programs.

Malta has two casinos offering a full range of gambling opportunities. The Dragonara Casino at the Westin Dragonara Hotel in St. Julian's, set in a huge Greek Revival style building, and the Oracle Casino at the New Dolmen Hotel in Qawra. The casinos open at noon and foreign nationals must be over 18 to enter. Take some identification with you.

Malta enjoys a healthy amount of theater, ballet and concert recitals particularly in the winter months. These are centered on venues in Valletta such as the Manoel Theater and the Astra Theater in Victoria, and take place at lunchtime or in the evening. The website of the Malta Tourist Authority <www.visitmalta.com> has a full list of activities taking place each month with contact details should you be interested in buying tickets.

BEACH ACTIVITIES

There are only a few sandy beaches on the Maltese islands whose coastlines are characterized by rocky outcrops and narrow inlets. The main beaches on Malta are found at Melleiha Bay in the north east, and Golden Bay in the southwest. Gozo has its best beach at Ramla Bay.

However, Malta is still popular with those who want to relax by spending time out in the sun. Lido pools with sun-

---

The festa

Each settlement in the Maltese islands has its own saint's day or *festa*. In the 72 hours leading up to the event, the population contemplates the coming day with prayers — it's a time to make amends or ask for the saints' help. The festa commences with a religious parade in which an effigy of the saint is carried through the streets. The community then takes part in a service at the parish church. Following this there's a village party with live music, dancing and huge firework displays. Visitors are very welcome to take part.

ning areas are cut into the rocks, thus providing seawater swimming pools in the summer months. These are popular with locals and visitors alike. Every coastal bay has platforms for sitting, and steps into the water to allow access for swimming and snorkelling.

Many large hotels will have two or three pool areas with sun decks, which take the place of the beach. Some have private beaches but these will not be fine sand.

Topless sunbathing is not permitted on public beaches but may be acceptable on private hotel beaches.

SPORTS

Malta offers facilities for a surprising number of sports and the climate is conducive to quite strenuous activities, especially in the spring and fall. Malta features an extensive regimen of competitive sporting events throughout the year, including cycle races, marathons, biathlons and triathlons. If you want to get involved yourself rather than being a spectator, Malta offers optimum conditions for the following sports.

Diving: The waters around Malta are some of the clearest in the Mediterranean with visibility between 40 and 50 m. This,

"In Guardia!"

Every second Sunday between September and May, Fort St. Elmo comes alive with the sound of clashing swords and musket fire in a historical parade and re-enactment called In Guardia!

It offers visitors an opportunity to step back in time to the era of the heroic Knights of Malta — to an age when the castle was new and perhaps the most impregnable in the world. The event is a breathtaking spectacle of color and noise starting at 11am. For exact dates contact the Malta Tourist Authority.

Unlocking the secrets of the deep: Scuba-diving around Malta offers some of the Mediterranean's best visibility.

along with a range of numerous natural features and wrecks to explore, make the islands popular destinations with divers and snorkellers. The waters can be a little cold early in the season, requiring dry suits to be worn, but the payoff is that these are often times of greatest visibility.

Maltese law requires that all divers must be over 14 years of age and have a medical certificate of fitness. Divers with less than PADI advanced certificate or equivalent must dive with a certified instructor.

Those who wish to dive independently will need a local dive permit. These are issued by the Malta Department of Health through your local dive center on Malta, Gozo or Comino.

If you wish to learn to dive in the Maltese islands there is an excellent network of dive centers, which offer training to professional levels. Centers are affiliated with one of the major certifying bodies with PADI (Professional Association of Diving Instructors) being the most common. The basic qualification, the Open Water certificate takes five days to complete. On completion this will allow you to dive with an instructor to a depth of 18 m (60 ft), which opens up many dive sites to you.

Protect yourself from Malta's strong sunshine.

St. Andrew's Dive Center, St. Simon Street, Xlendi offer an excellent service with a well-qualified staff and tailor-made dive boats. They are open all year round. Contact them; Tel. 2155 6441; fax 2156 1548; website <www.digi-gate .net/standrews>.

For any further information contact: The Federation of Underwater Activities; P.O. Box 29; Gzira GZR 10 Malta; Tel./fax 2131 4348.

Snorkelling: With so many rocky inlets, it's not surprising that the Maltese islands are a snorkellers heaven. The sea is clear and the fish plentiful, along with rock-dwelling creatures such as urchins and octopus.

Watersports: Most major hotels offer a full range of watersports, including jet skiing, windsurfing, sailing and inflatables. You can take lessons, or simply rent the equipment. The centers are generally open to non-guests.

Boat Rental: If you want to take to the water under your own steam, you can hire anything from a kayak to a ten berth "gin-palace." You'll need a skippers certificate for anything large — or you can hire a crew as part of the package and leave the hard work to them.

Tennis: Most hotels have at least one tennis court and these are often floodlit. Tennis is a very popular sport in Malta, with several communal court complexes in towns and villages.

Walking: With numerous country lanes to explore and high level of personal safety, Malta and particularly Gozo are perfect places for walking and hiking. The southwest areas of Malta and along the cliffs at Dingli take you to a rural Malta that you might otherwise not see on your visit. Many parts of Gozo have rural roadways where you can walk and much of the coastline remains unspoiled. Plans are afoot to put signs along pathways and produce walking maps. Until then, simply follow the main farming paths.

Cycling: The development of rugged mountain bikes has given cycling a new lease on life. Both Malta and Gozo are perfect places to explore, using the same paths as the walking trails.

Horseback-riding: Riding in the countryside can be very enjoyable. There are seven horse-riding centers in the islands. These can provide lessons or accompanied hacking along rural trails. S Darminin Riding Establishment 15, Sqaq L-Istalel, Marsa HMR 17; Tel. 2123 8507 (office) or 2123 5649 (stables) for details, have been in operation since 1948 and offer dressage, jumping and polo lessons in addition to hacking.

THINGS FOR CHILDREN

Malta has lots of attractions for children and they are made very welcome on the islands. Maltese children are treated with indulgence and will often be out late, especially on the long summer days, taking a stroll along the seafront with parents and grandparents, who will stop for a drink at a café or bar. These children will have had a long afternoon siesta in preparation for a late evening.

The sun is strong in Malta. Always make sure that children have skin protection at all times, even if they are playing in the water, and cover their heads with a hat.

Boat trips are always fun, whether it be across the Grand Harbor, out to the Blue Lagoon, or across to Gozo. There is still a wealth of sea life to look out for as you travel. A trip into the Blue Grotto or to the Inland Sea will fascinate them as they travel deep into the caves and watch the iridescent water shimmering and reflecting on the walls.

Take a *karrozin* ride around Valletta or Mdina. Children will enjoy being at the center of attention as they trot along, and can get high above the crowds for a better view.

The colorful and lively *festas* are perfect for children. There is lots of dancing and music, and no one seems to mind how much noise they make. Spectacular firework displays are a highlight. Just prepare the little ones for the accompanying noise.

Mediterraneo (see page 63) offers up-close interaction with pelicans, sea lions and dolphins with feeding and educational programs.

Popeye Village (see page 65) is a great place to explore, and is even more fun if you watch the film before you come.

The action of "In Guardia!" will fire your child's imagination about the past in a way that museums cannot.

What would a vacation be without dolphins? Thanks to the Mediterraneo sea life park, visitors need not find out.

Calendar of Events

Malta and Gozo have numerous events taking place throughout the year with the majority in the summer months. The number of separate festas is beyond the scope of the book — contact the Malta Tourist Authority for details of events taking place during your trip (website <www.visitmalta.com> has a comprehensive list under "Events") — but below is a list of the major events which happen throughout the year.

10 February: Feast of St. Paul's Shipwreck, with a procession in Valletta.

Carnival marking the beginning of Lent: Grotesque procession at Nadur on Gozo, and celebrations in most towns and villages.

Good Friday: Celebrated with a procession through the streets of Valletta (and other towns). Pageants in Rabat and Mosta.

31 March: Freedom Day. A nation-wide carnival, boat races in the Grand Harbor.

24–30 April: Malta History and Elegance. A week of pageants, re-enactments, music and dance.

29 June: Feast of St. Peter and St. Paul. The largest festa is at Nadur on Gozo.

15 August: Feast of the Assumption. Religious processions.

8 September: A celebration called Our Lady of Victories, marking the lifting of the sieges of 1565 and 1943. Boat races in the Grand Harbor; celebrations around Malta.

21 September: Independence Day. Official parades and fireworks displays.

6–8 October: The Mdina Festival. A range of activities and events in the city.

8 December: Feast of the Immaculate Conception is celebrated throughout the islands.

13 December: Republic Day, with celebrations around the island. Horseraces at Marsa.

EATING OUT

Maltese Specialties

Maltese cuisine is a fascinating amalgam of influences. Of great importance is the long relationship the people have had with the land — they know the crops that grow best, and when and where to grow them. The numerous overlords who have come and gone have also played their part, leaving behind them their particular ingredients and culinary techniques.

The climate is an important influence on Maltese cuisine. The spring season has ample rainfall that helps to ripen a number of fruits and vegetables (cabbage, cauliflowers, potatoes, onions, and citrus fruits). There is no rainfall in the summer months, but a sophisticated irrigation system allows a different range of crops to flourish (tomatoes, plums, melons, and grapes), and salad crops are harvested throughout most of the year. Thus the Maltese cook has always worked with the seasonal gluts of various fruits and vegetables — even with the advent of freezers for storage, they still prefer to use whatever is fresh and in season, making the seasonal dishes as their ancestors did.

Maltese dishes traditionally take time to prepare. This is for a number of reasons, but largely because the lack of wood for stoves and fires meant that creating a fire with a high heat was a false economy. In fact, until very recently many villages used a communal oven for hot dishes — this would have served as the village bakery — to make more economical use of the fuel. Because of this slow cooking method, many fine Maltese dishes do not transfer well to a restaurant menu, and this is in part why there are relatively few restaurants concentrating solely on Maltese food. Another reason is that the Maltese themselves have not traditionally eaten out at restaurants. Instead, they ate communally in extended family units. This tradition of the extended family getting together to eat still carries on in the present day — witness the huge family barbeques on beaches or at parks on Sundays. As the number of visitors began to grow, the Maltese simply opened restaurants serving what the visitors ate at home, hence the number of "international" menus to be found here. This is beginning to change and you can now find Maltese dishes on most restaurant menus.

The Gozitan diet typically includes fresh vegetables and freshly baked bread.

Even the very basics of Maltese cooking are excellent. Crusty bread is baked fresh every day — many settlements still have their own small bakeries so that people can purchase while it is still warm. This bread is then soaked in olive oil and smeared with tomato pulp, and is a staple lunch for many farmers and fishermen during their long working days. This simple dish called *hodz biz-zejt* is often served today as a pre–appetizer in restaurants. As an appetizer, *aljotta* (fish soup) is delicious, with its delicate lemon taste.

The land has historically provided a limited supply of protein. *Fenek* or rabbit is perhaps Malta's national meat and it is served in a number of ways. Most often you will find it on restaurant menus slow cooked in wine and garlic. Another popular method is fried in oil until it is crispy. Finally, you can eat rabbit meat and rabbit sauce with spaghetti, a way that Maltese housewives have traditionally made left-over rabbit stretch to another meal. Cheese has long been produced from sheep's milk (*gbejna*), and has a taste and texture like mozzarella. The Gozitans also produce an excellent goat cheese (*gbej-niet*), which they preserve with herbs, pepper, or sealed in a layer of olive oil. Of course the seas provided ample food in the form of fish, crustaceans, octopus, and squid, and you'll see what's been freshly caught sitting on ice in the restaurant. These will be weighed before cooking so that you will know the price. Mixed smaller fish will be served for a set price; these are steamed or fried. But this too is seasonal; the small boats could only set sail in the summertime. In winter the Mediterranean can be unforgiving — St. Paul's ship-

Seafood is much loved in Malta, and over the centuries, Maltese cooks have developed many ways of preparing it.

wreck is a clear example of this, and fish will give way to meat once again in homes and restaurants.

Maltese cooks over the centuries learned to make use of bountiful fruits and vegetables, so as to make a little meat or other protein go a long way. They preserved meat in sausages flavored with herbs and garlic, and mixed fish, meat or cheese with a variety of vegetables encased in pastry. *Lampuki* Pie, one of the most popular dishes, is dorado or *lampuka* fish and vegetables in pastry. *Pastizzi* is filo pastry boats filled with ricotta cheese. Pumpkin pie is a dish particular to Gozo.

Pasta is also used extensively here. Having traveled across from Sicily, pasta is considered as Maltese as it is Italian and housewives will still make it fresh several times each week. A favorite is *ravjul* or ravioli stuffed with cheese or mincemeat.

When not putting ingredients into pastry or pasta cases, Maltese cooks are stuffing them into other items. The Maltese love *bragjoli* or beef olives – thin beef fillets stuffed with a mincemeat, an onion and herb mixture, and smothered in an aromatic tomato-based sauce. Octopus (*qarnit mimli*) and squid (*calamari*) are stuffed, as are the abundant peppers, aubergines, and marrows. Ottoman Turkish rice, mincemeat, onions, and tomato sauce are particularly popular when stuffing vegetables. Equally popular is *rossfil-forn* — oven baked rice with mincemeat and tomato sauce. Another dish, *timpana*, is an interesting mixture of all three influences. A pastry pie filled with pasta — usually macaroni or penne — and a mixture of mincemeat, onions, and tomato sauce.

When the fall rains arrive and the fishermen pull their boats out of the water for the winter, the islands see an abundance of snails. Traditionally, the whole family would head out to collect them, to enjoy the short harvest. Today many restaurants make the most of the surplus by offering them as an appetizer, cooked in olive oil and garlic — even the left-over oil is great if you soak your Maltese bread in it! You can also find snails served in a sauce with pasta.

Sweets and Desserts

Traditional Maltese sweets and puddings have a distinctly eastern or Moorish influence. Many of these are served as finger foods rather than in plate sized portions, because they are so sweet. Try *imqaret* — dates in pastry deep-fried, or *biskuttini tal-lewz* — almond macaroons. *Helwa tat-Tork* is a sweetened mixture of whole and crushed almonds with sesame flour, and almonds are also used with candied fruit in nougat. *Kannoli*, deep fried pastry stuffed with ricotta cheese, chocolate and candied fruit arrived in the islands from Sicily.

Although very few restaurants will offer hot puddings, a popular winter dish in Maltese homes is bread pudding, cooking stale bread and dried fruits with a milk sauce flavoured with spices.

Malta also has a number of sweet foods, which are served only at festa time. Iced almond biscuits called *figolli* are produced only at Easter time, and *prinjolata* are sponge fingers with butter cream, almonds or pine nuts, decorated with chocolate and cherries.

International Cuisine

When Malta first began to expand its tourist industry, it concentrated on providing food that its visitors would find familiar. As a consequence, you will find a good range of different types of cuisine and high levels of quality. Many take full advantage of the fresh produce of the islands. You should not be disappointed by the quality of vegetables that accompany many entrée dishes, though the variety may disappoint after a while. Steaks can be found in many restaurants served with a range of sauces. Veal, *vitello*, is also popular. French "haute cuisine" is also available at a few of the more expensive restaurants.

You can eat in hundreds of trattoria-style restaurants offering a friendly informal atmosphere with pasta and pizza galore. Restaurateurs are increasingly using Maltese ingredients to give a different slant to pizzas — with Gozitan cheese or Maltese sausage — and pasta, such as serving it with rabbit instead of the usual *Bolognese* (mincemeat, and tomato) or *carbonara* (eggs, cream and ham) sauces.

The cafés in It-Tokk square provide an ideal spot to rest your tour-weary legs.

A few English pubs serve pies and fish and chips, though the Italian influence is beginning to overtake this last colonial influence. You can also find an increasing number of Chinese, and other south-east Asian restaurants, along with the odd Greek and Turkish restaurant or sushi bar.

Drinks

Coffee is strong and served in a range of Italian styles, especially espresso and cappuccino. Iced coffee is very popular in summer. Fruit juices are excellent and refreshing, especially on long summer days. Most are freshly produced on the premises. The Maltese also produce their own soft drink called Kinnie — a sparkling orange drink flavoured with herbs — but also have a full range of international soft drinks too.

A Maltese barman instinctively takes pleasure in pouring a pint of Cisk, a refreshing domestic beer.

You will find two types of domestic beer, both lager types. Cisk, pronounced *Chisk*, is the lighter, Hopleaf is still refreshing but has a slightly heavier, nuttier taste.

The island produces a range of wines, which have improved greatly over the last 20 years. The Marsovin winery has invested heavily in new machinery and techniques, taking advice from French and Californian growers. Grapes imported from Sicily supplement home-grown varieties. La Vallette is the brand name of a very acceptable table wine, which compliments many Maltese and Italian dishes. Single varietal wines such as Merlot and Sauvignon Blanc add to the range available. Italian and French wines are imported in great variety to supplement the domestic brands.

For after dinner drinks, two unusual liqueurs are produced on Malta. Bajtra — said to be the favorite after dinner "tipple" of the Knights — is made by distilling the juice of the prickly

pear, imparting an interesting purple hue to the finished drink.
The second, Tamakari is a sweet-flavored clear liqueur.

Help with the Menu

The list below contains a selection of the words (Maltese, Italian,
and French) that you might come across on a Maltese menu.

abbachio, agnello, agneau	lamb
aglio, ail	garlic
anitra, canard	duck
boeuf, manzo	beef
braġoli, bragioli	beef olive
carciofi, qaqoċċ	artichoke
ċerna	grouper fish (*mérou*)
coniglio, lapin, fenek	rabbit
dolce	dessert
espadon, pesce spada	swordfish
fagioli, fagiolini, haricots	beans
formaggio, fromage	cheese
funghi, champignons	mushrooms
ġbejna	Maltese sheep's milk
homard, astice	lobster
lampuka	dolphinfish special to Malta
melanzana	aubergine, eggplant
naranja	orange
patate, pommes de terre	potatoes
pesce, poisson	fish
piselli, perits pois	peas
prosciutto, jambon	ham
salsa	sauce
pâtes	pasta
tonn, tonno, thon	tuna (tunny)
uove, oeufs	eggs
vongole	clams

HANDY TRAVEL TIPS

An A–Z Summary of Practical Information

A

ACCOMMODATION

There is a full range of accommodation in Malta, from five-star hotels to a wide range of self-catering options. All establishments offering accommodation are classified by the Maltese Hotel and Catering Establishments Board (HCEB) against a pre-determined set of criteria conforming to that of international standards. Standards of service are also rated, from De Luxe (the highest standard), to Gold, to Bronze (the lowest). The web site <www.travel-malta.com> is a useful Internet booking service.

Hotels: Hotels are classified from one to five stars. Hotels in class one or two will not be guaranteed to have rooms with private facilities. Always make inquiries before making a firm booking. Hotels in the higher star ratings will be well-equipped. Prices are normally quoted per person per night. When room rates are quoted, they include continental breakfast. High season, when prices are highest, is from mid-July to the end of September. Low season is from November to the end of March, however prices will rise at Christmas and Easter. About 20% of Malta's tourists visit in the winter season, a great many of these travel on vacation packages from Europe.

Many hotels offer full board for relatively little extra money, however eating out is inexpensive in the islands.

Self-catering options: Self-catering is a popular choice by visitors to Malta. These can be simple studios or apartments in small blocks, apart-hotels which offer some hotel-style accommodation and some units with kitchens, self-catering vacation complexes with restaurants, pools, etc., or renovated farmhouses set out in the countryside — a particular favorite on Gozo. Two self-catering vacation complexes which offer a full range of facilities (pools, gym, restaurants, etc.) are: Corinthia Mistra Village Clubhotel, Xemxija Hill, St. Paul's Bay SPB 15; Tel. 2158 0481; fax 2158 2941; web site <www.

corinthiahotels. com> and Mellieha Holiday Centre, Mellieha Bay, Mellieha SPB 15; Tel. 2157 3900; fax 2157 5452. For farmhouse rentals on Gozo try Gozo Great Escapes, 22 Triq it-Torri Gauci, Naxxar, Malta; Tel. 2141 9505; fax 2141 9406; web site <www. vol.net.mt/com/gozoescape>

AIRPORT

Gudja International Airport serves the whole of the archipelago. It was opened in 1992 and is 10 km (6 m) south-east of Valletta. You will find airline ticketing offices, exchange facilities, car rental offices, a chapel, tourist information bureau, and bars and restaurants here. For flight enquiries Tel. 2124 9600 or 2169 7800.

Taxis are available outside the arrivals terminal for the short journey into town; buy a voucher inside the terminal and present it to the driver.

B

BICYCLE RENTAL

Bicycling is easy and fun, particularly on Gozo with its quieter roads. All-terrain bikes offer the chance to take to the country tracks away from the towns. Contact Lillywhites, St. George's Road, St. Julian's, Malta; Tel. 2133 5921 or Victor Sultana, New Building, Main Gate Street, Victoria, Gozo; Tel. 2155 6414.

BUDGETING FOR YOUR TRIP

Malta and Gozo are inexpensive destinations by European standards with food, excursions, and attractions offering good value for money. Here are a few sample prices to help you with your budgeting.

Car Rental: small vehicle per week Lm 80 per week in August.

Entrance fee for State Museums: Lm 1.

Commercial attractions: approximately Lm 3–5 for adults.

Dinner for one without drinks in a moderate restaurant: Lm 8–10.

Room rate per person/per night for a medium room: Lm 18–25 per person/per night. Full board may be as little as Lm 5 extra.

Horse and buggy tour: Lm 3 for the first 30 minutes.

Island Tour by bus: Lm 6 per person.

Harbour Boat Tour: Lm 6 per person.

Open Water dive course: Lm 100 for one accompanied dive; Lm 7 for full equipment rental for the day.

C

CAR RENTAL

Car rental is on par with most other European countries. In August, a small car will cost around Lm 80 per week. A car will free you from the strictures of the bus timetable or tour itinerary, but driving and navigating around the island is a challenge. Collision damage waiver is expensive (around Lm 6 per day) but will be worth it for the peace of mind. Always check with your credit card or domestic insurance provider as you may be insured through your existing policies.

All the major car-rental companies — Hertz, Avis, and Europcar — have offices on the island; however, some are run as franchises rather than as main branches. Some have desks at the airport, and it is possible to pick up a car immediately upon your arrival. Some of the larger rental companies offer more competitive rates if you reserve the car from home.

Here are the contact details of the major rental companies.

Avis local head office Tel. 2124 6640; fax 2123 5754; web site <www.avis.com>.

Hertz local head office Tel. 2131 4636; fax 2133 3153; local web site <www.hertz.com.mt>.

Europcar local head office Tel. 2138 8516; fax 2137 3673; local web site <www.europcar.com>.

If you decide to hire a car while in Malta, a reliable local company is Merlin Car Hire, Merlin House, Triq Mountbatten, Hamrun; Tel. 2122 3131; fax 2122 1321; web site <www.merlin.com.mt>.

Malta

If you rent in Malta there is no problem with taking your car to Gozo on the ferry.

The condition of the vehicles is good. Most companies have age limits between 25 and 70. Your national licence will be acceptable and you will need to show it when you pick up the car.

CAMPING
There are no organized campsites on any of the islands.

CLIMATE
Malta has a typical Mediterranean climate with hot, dry summers and mild, humid winters. Even in the winter months many days have long bouts of sunshine. The short spring is characterized by sunny days with cool breezes. By May the rain ceases until October and the temperature begins to rise quickly. In spring, flowers and crops cover the terraced farming areas, but by the end of the harvest in May, the land becomes parched and is almost bare by the middle of summer. Summer heat is exacerbated by warm winds from North Africa, but the situation is mitigated by sea breezes, which cool off the coastal areas.

Air temperature		J	F	M	A	M	J	J	A	S	O	N	D
Average daily	°F	59	60	62	66	71	82	83	84	82	67	69	63
maximum*	°C	15	15	16	19	23	27	30	31	28	24	20	17
Average daily	°F	49	49	51	54	59	65	70	71	69	63	57	53
minimum*	°C	19	19	10	12	15	19	21	22	20	17	14	11
Water temperature	°F	58	58	58	62	65	70	75	76	77	72	67	62
	°C	14	14	14	16	18	21	24	26	25	22	19	16

* Maximum temperatures are measured in the early afternoon, minimum temperatures just before sunrise.

CLOTHING
Malta has long, hot, sunny days from early May until the end of September. If you are traveling at this time, T-shirts, light shirts, shorts, and slacks or light dresses make ideal clothing. Don't forget a hat and sunglasses.

You'll need swimwear for the beach or pool, but it isn't considered acceptable to walk around town in swimwear.

If traveling in spring or fall, take a couple of extra layers of clothing — warmer trousers and a sweater or jacket for chillier days (it can be breezy early or late in the season), and to wear in the evenings when it can get cooler. In winter, a layer of warm clothing is advised, plus protection against the rain.

In the evenings casual attire is acceptable in most establishments. However, if you intend to eat at some of the finer restaurants, a jacket for men (ties are rarely required) and 'dressy' ensemble for women is appropriate — make inquiries on dress code when you book.

If you intend to visit any of the churches around the islands you will need to make sure that you are appropriately dressed. This means no shorts for men, and both sexes must have their shoulders covered. Take off hats when entering a church.

COMPLAINTS

In the first instance, complaints should be taken up with the establishment concerned. If you are still dissatisfied and if your complaint is with either a hotel or restaurant, approach the Hotel and Catering Establishments Board who license all such businesses Tel. 2124 2919. For all other complaints contact the Malta Tourism Authority, they should be able to direct you to the appropriate body to advise you further.

CRIME AND SAFETY

Malta is still relatively crime-free compared to the rest of the world. However, petty crime such as theft is on the increase in tourist areas and it pays to take precautions against becoming a victim. Put your valuables in the hotel safe if there is one. Don't carry large amounts of cash and don't leave valuables unattended on beaches or visible in your vehicle. Walk only on well-lit streets at night.

If you do become a victim of crime, you should report this to the police immediately.

CUSTOMS AND ENTRY REQUIREMENTS

Entry Requirements: The following nationalities do not need an entry visa for stays of under three months: Australia, Canada, New Zealand, Republic of Ireland, South Africa, United Kingdom, and the United States. If a trip is to be extended past three months, a written request must be made to the Commissioner of Police, Police Headquarters, Floriana before the end of the three-month period.

Currency restrictions: There is no limit to the amount of foreign currency that can be imported into Malta, provided that it is declared upon arrival. The maximum amount of Maltese currency that can be imported into Malta is Lm 50 per person. No more than Lm 25 per person may be exported. An exchange slip will be needed to change Lm currency back into foreign currency on departure. Customs officials have the right to search and question departing passengers with regard to currency on their person. Carry your exchange slip or ATM receipt with you in the unlikely event of being questioned.

Customs: Belongings for personal use are exempt from duty. Other duty-free allowances upon entry (for those staying in Malta for longer than 24 hours) are: 10 ml of perfume, 125 ml of toilet water. For all travelers: 200 cigarettes or 100 cigarillos or 50 cigars or 250 g of tobacco, one liter of spirits and one liter of wine for each person over the age of 17 years.

It is advisable to declare any large or unusual items such as expensive cameras, or laptop computers on arrival. These will then be cleared on your departure.

DRIVING

Driving can be viewed as an adventure or a nightmare, depending on your point of view. It is not for the faint of heart but can be immensely rewarding since you can make your own timetable and visit the major sites when the large tour groups have departed. General points to remember are the poor driving ability and the sheer number of vehicles. Lane discipline is poor; cars will pull out of junctions in front of you or turn off without using indicators (turn signals); traveling through red lights is common, as is stopping on traffic circles when they have right of way. Vehicles will often pull out to pass a line of parked cars totally blocking your side of the road and leaving you with nowhere to go. Vehicles are often in poor condition resulting in poor acceleration, noise, and belching exhaust fumes.

Road signs for the major attractions are intermittent, and many streets look exactly the same to the untrained eye, which makes map-reading a challenge. Having said that, Malta is such a small island that you are never lost, you may simply find yourself somewhere where you didn't expect to be. There is little to fear about security and most local people are approachable and only too happy to point you in the right direction.

If you are bringing in your own car don't forget your driver's license and registration documents.

Road Conditions: Driving is on the left with passing on the right, as in the UK. Roads have not yet been given official classifications but on most maps should appear either red (a major road), yellow (a secondary road), or white (a country road). Road conditions vary enormously. The major roads can be good but are prone to subsidence in coastal areas. Minor or country roads can be very poor with numerous potholes. A few white roads will be dirt tracks but this is becoming rare on Malta. Always use caution even on what appears to be a good stretch of road, and prepare for the unexpected.

On the main highway around the capital, exits can be on the left or right and can be very tight, with short runs on or off the main roadway.

Rules and Regulations: There are speed limits of 65 kph (40 mph) on highways, 40 kph (25 mph) in urban areas, though many local people do not abide by the law and drive higher than the limit. One must also always be prepared to travel at much slower speeds on country lanes. Be constantly vigilant of other road users. Drivers and front-seat passengers must use seat belts; rear-seat passengers must also use seat belts if they are available. Motorcycle riders must wear a crash helmet.

In most towns and villages there are one-way systems making a direct route through town impossible. This tests navigation skills.

If you are involved in an accident, call the police (Tel. 191) and do not move your vehicle until they arrive. Although this causes mayhem for other road users, it is important to obtain a police report to settle any claims that may arise from traffic incidents.

Fuel Costs: Fuel costs around 35c per liter for unleaded. Diesel is around half this price, hence the popularity of diesel vehicles. Fuel stations are open from Mon–Sat 7am–6pm in winter, 7am–7pm in summer. On Sundays they open on a rota system — look for details in the local press. They do accept credit cards for payment and an increasing number are installing automatic dispensing machines for credit card transactions.

Parking: There seem to be many more vehicles than parking spaces, especially in the main tourist resorts and the capital. Street parking is allowed provided there are no posted restrictions — these include residents-only parking. A yellow line at the side of the road means no parking. Most of the new larger hotels have parking lots for guest vehicles but smaller, older ones may not. Although leaving a car on the street is not a problem as far as security is concerned (don't leave valuables in your car), being able to find a suitable parking space near your hotel could be.

Parking in Valletta itself is difficult. There is a large underground parking lot near the bus station, and parking by City Gate or along the city wall by Marsamxett Harbor. It is best to leave the car at one of these places and enter the city on foot.

Most of the major sites outside Valletta have a parking area. These are often manned by unofficial "parking attendants" wearing peaked hats, who will orchestrate your arrival and departure in exchange for a small sum — carry small change for this purpose.

If You Need Help: There are many mechanics on Malta who will tow your vehicle and make on-the-spot repairs at an inexpensive price. However, it would be advisable to speak to your car rental agency about who to contact in such an eventuality.

Road Signs: Malta uses international road signals, and many will be instantly understandable. Official signs will be in English.

E

ELECTRICITY
The electrical supply is 240 volts/50 cycles and the British style 3 pin, 13 ampere socket is standard.

EMBASSIES/CONSULATES/HIGH COMMISSIONS
There is diplomatic representation on Malta for the following countries.
Australia: Australian High Commission; Villa Florientina; Ta'Xbiex Terrace; Ta'Biex; Tel. 2133 8210; fax 2134 4059.

New Zealand: Consulate; Villa Hampstead; Oliver Agius Street; Attard.; Tel. 2143 5025.

UK: High Commission; 7, St. Anne Street, Floriana; Tel. 2123 3134; fax 2124 2001.

US: Embassy; 3rd Floor, Development House; St. Anne Street; Floriana; Tel. 2123 5960; fax 2124 3229.

For the following countries, the nearest diplomatic mission is in Rome, Italy.

Canada: Embassy, Consular Section; Via Zara 30; 00198 Rome; Tel. 00 39 06 445981; fax 44598912.

Republic of Ireland: Embassy of the Republic of Ireland; Piazza di Campitelli 3 (Scalla A, Int 2); 00186 Rome; Tel. 00 39 06 6979121.

South Africa: South African Embassy; Via Tanaro 14; 00198 Rome; Tel. 00 39 06 852541; fax 84242237.

EMERGENCIES

The emergency telephone numbers are:

    196 for ambulance.
    199 for fire or crime.
    191 for traffic accidents.

GAY AND LESBIAN TRAVELERS

Malta is a conservative destination and same-sex relationships would be shocking for many residents, however there will be no violent undertone and there are a small number of gay-friendly bars in the resort areas of Sliema and St. Julian's.

GETTING THERE

By Air: The national carrier for the islands is Air Malta. It operates a comprehensive number of services to Europe and North Africa, and has regular flight connections with the following cities–London Heathrow/Gatwick/Stansted, Glasgow, Birmingham and Manchester in the UK; Dublin and Cork in the Republic of Ireland; Amsterdam, Brussels, Paris, Geneva, Frankfurt, and Rome. All of these connections allow for easy onward travel from destinations in the US (it has partnership agreements with TWA via London Gatwick or Milan Malpensa), Canada, South Africa, Australia and New Zealand. As a guideline, flying times from London are around three hours. Air Malta flight schedules can be accessed on <www.airmalta.com>.

Other airlines that operate scheduled services to Malta include: British Airways, Alitalia, and Lufthansa.

Gozo has no airport but has a helipad and Malta Air Charter, an Air Malta subsidiary company, operates a regular helicopter service between the two islands from Malta International Airport.

Charter operations: Malta is a popular destination from many European countries, and a large number of operators fly to the island all year round, with an increased number of flights during the summer months. These can be booked flights only or with hotels/self-catering accommodations as part of the package. The main companies that operate from the UK are Air 2000, Air UK, Airtours, and Thomson. Malta Direct, a subsidiary of Air Malta, also offers flights and packages.

By Sea: Malta is linked by regular ferry services with mainland Italy, the island of S 73; web site <www.grimaldi-ferries.com>. MaReSi Shipping operates a service between Malta and Reggio Calabria. Tel: 2123 3129; website <www.sms.com.mt>.

By Car: If you travel with your own vehicle no bond is required in order to enter Malta, as long as you are planning to stay for less than three months. A Green Card will be necessary — this extends your insurance coverage so that your vehicle is covered 3rd party while you are overseas — and can be obtained through your national motoring or touring organization. You may need to sign a declaration that you do not intend to sell the vehicle while travelling in Malta.

By Train: Rail services also connect with the ferries so it is possible to travel by rail to Genoa or Reggio Calabria and travel as a foot passenger on the ferry to Malta. Details of ticket prices and schedules can be obtained from the Eurorail web site <www.eurorail.com>.

A number of cruise lines offer Malta on their itinerary of Mediterranean cruises. These include Fred Olsen Lines, Holland America Line, Royal Caribbean, Cunard, and P & O.

GUIDES AND TOURS
A number of reliable companies offer daily tours around the island or to Gozo. These normally include a guide, but the quality of guides varies. The Malta Tourism Authority licenses a number of guides for itineraries. Contact them for more details.

Malta

Captain Morgan Cruises offer a full program of tours by air, sea or on land. Contact them at: Dolphin Court, Tigné Seafront, Sliema; Tel. 2134 3373; fax 2133 2004; web site <www.captainmorgan.com.mt>.

Gozo Explorer offers tailor-made Jeep tours of the island, catering for specific interests or just general sightseeing. They can be contacted at 26 Comino Street, Ghajnsielem, Gozo; Tel. 2156 1010; e-mail <maltesefalcon@orbit.net.mt>.

HEALTH AND MEDICAL CARE
Health concerns: There are no serious health concerns to worry about when you visit Malta. In summer the sun is strong, and even early or late in the season it is sensible to take precautions. To avoid it, limit your time in the sun during your first few days, apply regular protection products, and carry clothing to cover your skin should it begin to burn. A hat and sunglasses are important. Don't forget that the effects of the sun can penetrate water — so you still need protection in the pool or the sea. Always make sure that young children are adequately protected while playing. Mosquitoes can be a problem; always carry insect repellent with you and apply it regularly when you need to and especially in the evenings.

The standard of general medical facilities is good and all medical personnel speak excellent English. There is one general hospital on Malta and one on Gozo. There are also several health centers open 24 hours a day for minor health problems/accidents. In an emergency dial 196 for medical assistance.

St. Luke's Hospital, Guardamangia, Malta; Tel. 24 12 51.
Gozo General Hospital, Ghajn Qatet Street, Victoria; Tel. 56 16 00.

Vaccinations: No vaccinations are normally needed except if you are arriving from a cholera- or yellow fever-infected area and are within 6 days of leaving that area.

Water: Although it is safe to drink it does not always taste pleasant, so bottled water is advised.

Insurance: A comprehensive insurance policy covering accidents and illness among other items is recommended. This will cover the cost of emergency treatment, aftercare, or repatriation.

Emergency treatment: Malta has reciprocal health agreements with the UK and Australia. Nationals from these countries who stay less than one month and six months respectively will receive free health treatment.

A range of 'over-the-counter' drugs is available for everyday ailments and chemists (pharmacists) will be able to advise you on minor ailments. Most prescription drugs are available on the islands. A letter from your doctor will be needed for a prescription to be issued by a Maltese doctor. Chemists are open during normal store hours with a few Sunday openings (check the local press).

HITCHHIKING

Hitchhiking is not illegal but it is not common (probably because bus fares are so cheap) and should be avoided in the heat of the summer days. Although Malta is a very safe country, hitchhiking has its inherent dangers, and women traveling alone should take great care.

HOLIDAYS

The following dates are public holidays. Tourist shops and restaurants will probably not be closed, but local shops, offices and banks will be.

Where a holiday falls on a Saturday or Sunday, the following Monday may be taken as the official holiday.

Public holidays in Malta and Gozo are:

1 January — New Years Day.

10 February — St. Paul's Shipwreck Day

19 March — St. Joseph's Day

31 March — Freedom Day

Malta

Good Friday, Easter Sunday, and Easter Monday

1 May — Labor Day

7 June — Commemoration of 7th June 1919 (Sette Guigno)

29 June — St. Peter and St. Paul Day (L'Imanarja)

15 August — Assumption

8 September — Victory Day

21 September — Independence Day

8 December — Feast of the Immaculate Conception

13 December — Republic Day

25 December — Christmas Day

26 December — Public Holiday

L

LANGUAGE

There are two official languages in Malta, Maltese or Malti — an ancient form spoken language related to Arabic and written in the Roman script — and English which is spoken fluently by most of the population. Many street names and signs in major towns are printed in Malti and English but not all, so it helps to have a basic understanding of how certain letters and words are pronounced. This will certainly help you when you are asking for directions.

ċ	–	like *ch* in *ch*ild
g	–	as in *g*ood
ġ	–	like *j* in *j*ob
għ	–	silent, unless at the end of a word (*h* as in *h*ello)
h	–	silent, unless at the end of a word (*h* as in *h*ello)
ħ	–	*h*
j	–	like *y* in *y*ear; **aj** like *igh* in h*igh*; **ej** like *ay* in s*ay*
q	–	almost silent—like a very faint *kh*-sound; a bit like cockney glottal stop "ain't i*t*"

x – like *sh* in *sh*op

z – *ts*

ż – *z*

A Few Everyday Expressions:

	Maltese	pronunciation
good morning	**bonġu**	BON-joo
good evening	**bonswa**	BON-swah
yes	**iva**	EE-vah
no	**le**	leh
please	**jek jogħġbok**	yehekYOJ-bok
thank you	**grazzi**	GRAHT-see
excuse me	**skużi**	SKOO-zee
Where is ...?	**Fejn hu ...?**	fayn oo
right	**lemin**	LEH-meen
left	**xellug**	shehl-LOOG
straight ahead	**dritt il-quddiem**	drit il-KHOOD-dee-ehm
How much?	**Kemm?**	kehm

Ta' means "the place of"

Numbers:

0	**Xejn**	shayn
1	**Wieħed**	WEE-hehd
2	**Tnejn**	tnayn
3	**Tlieta**	TLEE-tah
4	**Erbgħa**	EHR-bah
5	**Ħamsa**	Hum-sah
6	**Sitta**	SIT-tah
7	**Sebgħa**	SEH-bah
8	**Tmienja**	TMEE-ehn-yah
9	**Disgħa**	DIS-sah
10	**Għaxra**	AHSH-rah

Malta

Common Town and Site Names:

The Maltese like to hear at least their town names pronounced properly. So here's a list of the main sites mentioned in this book.

Birżebbuġa	beer-zeeb-BOO-jah
Borġ in-Nadur	borj in nah-DOOR
Buġibba	Boo-JIB-ba
Ġgantija	J'GAHN-tee-yah
Għar Dalam	ahr DAH-lam
Għar Ħassan	ahr hahs-SAHN
Għar Lapsi	ahr LAHP-see
Għarb	ahrb
Ħaġar Qim	hah-jahr-khEEM
Marsamxett	mahr-sahm-SHEHTT
Marsaxlokk	mahr-sash-LOKK
Mdina	im-DEE-nah
Mġarr	im-JAHRR
Naxxar	NAHS-shahr
Qala	khAH-lah
Qawra	khOW-rah
Qormi	khOHR-mee
Siġġiewi	SEEJ-jee-eh-wee
Tarxien	TAHR-sheen
Xagħra	SHAH-rah
Xlendi	SHLEHN-dee
Żebbuġ	ZEHB-booj
Żejtun	ZAY-toon

LAUNDRY AND DRY CLEANING

All four and five star hotels are required to have laundry and dry-cleaning on site. However if you want to use a private, commercial organization, Swan has a number of sites throughout Malta with a free phone number (Tel. 0800 776614) for door-to-door delivery.

 M

MAPS

The Malta Tourism Authority prints a number of maps and short guides that are perfect for exploring the major towns on the islands on foot. If you require a map that is suitable for touring by car, there is a range available from tourist shops around the islands. None has comprehensive coverage of the one way systems in each settlement but will be helpful from getting from place to place. Try the Marco Polo Leisure Map, which is available in most tourist shops.

MEDIA

Newspapers: The main English newspapers for the island are the Malta Times and The Independent. Both concentrate on local political and domestic issues, covering world news in brief. Most major hotels and newsagents sell the major British dailies on the days they are printed. The International Herald Tribune is also available, but major US newspapers are more difficult to find and will be one day old.

TV: Most hotels will offer a news channel such as CNN as part of their media service, along with the BBC, German, Italian, French and Arabic channels.

MONEY

Cash: The official currency of Malta and Gozo is the Maltese Lira, abbreviated to Lm and often called pounds by older local people (this goes back to the use of the British pound sterling on the island before independence in 1964). Each Lira is divided into one hundred cents and each cent into ten mils (no longer used today as they are worth very little).

Notes are printed in Lm2, Lm5, Lm10, Lm20; coins in 1c, 2c, 5c, 10c, 25c, 50c, and Lm1.

Malta

There is no limit to the amount of foreign currency that can be imported into Malta, provided that it is declared on arrival. The maximum amount of Maltese currency that can be imported into Malta is Lm 50 per person. No more than Lm 25 per person may be exported. An exchange slip will be needed to change Lm currency back into foreign currency before your departure. Customs officials have the right to search and question departing passengers with regard to currency on their person. Carry your exchange slip or ATM receipt with you in the unlikely event of being questioned.

Currency Exchange: Currency can be exchanged at banks, government accredited currency bureaux, hotels and some shops. Banks offer the best exchange rates.

ATMs and credit cards: A large number of banks have ATMs which accept international debit cards — look for the Cirrus or Plus cards' sign on the machine. Most machines will also dispense cash against major credit cards. Some machines will impose an extra charge on withdrawals on foreign banks. Credit cards are widely accepted throughout the islands in hotels, shops, and restaurants. You will even be able to buy goods from some market stalls with credit cards. An increasing number of businesses can also accept payment by international debit card (Maestro); you will see signs in the window advertising the facility.

Travelers' checks: Most hotels, and many major stores, are happy to accept travelers' checks in payment. You can also cash travelers' checks at banks and hotels.

OPEN HOURS

Opening hours in Malta, as in many Mediterranean countries, can be complicated. Winter hours are longer than those in summer when the heat becomes oppressive in the afternoons. Generally longer working days begin on 1 October and end on 16 June. If you have any important business to attend to, it would be advisable to do it in the mornings when banks, offices, shops, and government buildings will definitely be open.

All commercial activity stops at lunchtime whatever time of year it is; even major churches are closed so that the Maltese can observe the tradition of a substantial midday meal and afternoon siesta.

Banks: Different banks have slightly varying opening hours, but as a general guide they are open from Mon–Fri 8am–12:45pm, Sat 8–11.30am, plus Friday afternoons 2.30–4pm. Main branches open Mon–Fri 4–7pm..

Government offices: From 16 June–30 Sept they are open Mon–Fri 7:30am–1:30pm. From 1 Oct–15 June 7:45am–12:30pm and 1:15pm–5:15pm.

Commercial offices: From 1 July–30 Sept, Mon–Fri 7:30am–1:30pm. 1 Oct–30 June, 8:30am–1pm and 3pm–5:30pm.

Shops: Mon–Fri 9am–1pm and 4pm–7pm, Sat 9am–1pm. Many shops in tourist areas do not close for lunch and are open longer hours, especially in summer. Sunday opening is gradually catching on.

Museums: Museums are generally open on Mon–Sat from 8.15am–5pm, Sun 7.45am–2pm (see page 78 for more details).

 P

POLICE

The police in Malta are friendly and approachable, and they will certainly offer assistance if you are lost. They wear blue uniforms in the summer, and black (with peaked caps) in winter. Police vehicles are blue-and-white. Some officers may travel by scooter; these have no official markings. There are police stations in each major town but some are not manned 24 hours a day. For a crime emergency: Tel. 199. Always report traffic accidents to the police and do not move your vehicle until they arrive. To report traffic accidents, use Tel. 191.

Police headquarters are at St. Calcidonius Square, Floriana, Malta; Tel. 2122 40 01 or 2122 40 02.

On Gozo 2156 20 40.

For ambulance: Tel. 196.

POST OFFICES

Malta has a relatively efficient postal system; usual opening hours are Mon–Sat 7.30am–12.45pm. The post offices at 305 Qormi Road, Qormi and at the airport are open Mon–Sat 8am–6:30pm.

In Gozo the main office is at 129 Republic Street, Victoria; opening hours are Mon–Sat 7.30am–12.45pm.

Post boxes are located in street-side locations and are painted red. They may either be inserted into the wall or round free-standing structures. Most hotels will post cards for you. The price of a stamp is 15c for Europe, 25c for US, Aus, NZ and SA.

PUBLIC TRANSPORTATION

Buses: The local bus service on Malta is comprehensive, reliable and cheap — a maximum of 30c for the longest journey. Most buses are 1950s and 1960s models, lovingly cared for and kept in pristine livery — a pretty orange color. Bus services start from a central hub just outside City Gate in Valletta and operate on a fixed schedule. A Malta Bus Map is available (current price 25c) from the travel information kiosk in the bus station. This gives all route numbers and destinations, shows where the bus stop for each number is located in the station, and gives the current pricing structure for journeys. Day tickets are available up to a maximum of a 7-day ticket. The price for this is Lm 4 per person. These can be bought from Bank of Valletta branches throughout the island.

Gozo buses have a terminus at Main Gate Street in Victoria. They are colored grey. The buses operate on a circular route with no fixed timetable. A service connects with the ferry timetable to allow you to reach Victoria easily on your arrival on the island. Fares are a maximum of 9c per person per journey.

Taxis: The white taxis are fitted with meters and should charge government-controlled rates that should be on display in the cab. If a driver is reluctant to use his meter, agree on a price before starting your journey. Taxis can be hired per hour. This could be a good option for touring out of the city if you don't want to drive.

Ferry: The Marsamxetto Steamferry Service, Dolphin Court, Tigné Sea Front; Tel. 2133 1961; fax 2133 4420 operates a passenger only service between Sliema and Valletta. This operates Mon–Sat at a cost of 35c one way.

Horse drawn buggies *(karrozin)*: These offer tours rather than journeys. Official fares are Lm3 for 30 minutes and 75c for each subsequent 30 minutes, however these are rarely enforced and a fare should be agreed before you start your journey. You will find them in Valletta, Mdina, and Sliema.

Between the islands

Air: Malta Air Charter, Gudja International Airport; Tel. 2166 2211; fax 2166 3195; web site <www.airmalta.com> operates a helicopter service from Gudja International Airport to the heliport at Xewkija on Gozo several times each day.

Sea: The Gozo Channel Company, Hey Wharf, Sa Maison; Tel. 2124 3964; fax 2124 8007 operates passenger catamarans and vehicle ferries from Sa Maison (west of Valletta) and Ċirkewwa (on the western tip of Malta) to Mġarr on Gozo every morning and evening. There is also a ferry service that runs every 30 minutes during the day and hourly through the night.

The Comino Hotel has a ferry boat, which provides transportation to both Malta and Gozo.

Private boats offer tours of Gozo or the Blue Lagoon on Comino from Ċirkewwa or resorts along the northern coastline of Malta. Many operate in summer only.

R

RELIGION

The Maltese population is predominantly Roman Catholic but there are Anglican, Baptist, Buddhist, Jehovah's Witness, Jewish, Methodist, Mormon, Muslim, and Orthodox places of worship on Malta.

T

TELEPHONE

The international country code for Malta and Gozo is 356 followed by the number.

When making an international call always dial 00 before the country code.

International codes are as follows:

US and Canada: 1	*Ireland*: 353
UK: 44	*New Zealand*: 64
South Africa: 27	*Australia*: 61

Maltacom is the provider of all land line services in the islands. Most hotels will offer direct-dial long distance and international phone facilities, but these can be priced at a premium, which can be extremely expensive. Maltacom has a 24 hour office offering calling, faxing, and e-mail facilities at Mercury House, St. George's Road, Paceville; Tel. 2131 0980.

Phone calls, including international calls, can be made from call boxes and kiosks using coins, credit cards, and calling cards, although older boxes may only accept coins. Phone cards of various denominations can be purchased from newsagents, post offices, and drug stores.

TIME ZONES

Malta operates on Central European Time (CET), which is one hour ahead of Greenwich Mean Time in winter and two hours ahead between the end of March and the end of October.

Malta is six hours ahead of Eastern Standard Time (EST) in winter, seven in summer.

In summer the following times apply:

New York	London	**Valletta**	Jo'burg	Sydney	Auckland
6:00 A.M.	11:00 A.M.	**noon**	noon	8:00 P.M.	10:00 P.M.

TIPPING

Tipping for good service is expected in Malta. Some restaurants will include a service charge in the final bill but most will not. If service charge has not already been included, 10-12% is usual.

The following other guidelines apply:

Taxi driver: 10%

Porters: 15c per piece of luggage.

Maids: 30-40c per day.

TOILETS

Malta has public toilets in most major towns — in market squares, harbors, or near bus stations — although cleanliness varies. Malta's museums and historical sites are all striving to provide facilities even if they are in the form of portable toilets. You can use the facilities in bars. If there is an attendant, a small tip would be appropriate.

TOURIST INFORMATION

The Malta Tourism Authority (MTA) is responsible for tourist information and they have a number of excellent leaflets and brochures to help visitors make the most of their trip.

The head office of the organization also acts as a center for information during your stay on the island.

Malta

Auberge d'Italie
Merchants Street
Valletta CMR 02, Malta.
Tel. 2191 5000; Fax: 2191 5893
web site <www.tourism.org.mt>

MTA also has offices in the following countries:

UK and Ireland: Malta Tourist Office; Malta House; 36-38 Piccadilly; London W1J 0LD; Tel. 020-7292 4900; web site <www.visitmalta.com>.

US and Canada: Malta National Tourist Office; Empire State Building; 350 Fifth Avenue, Suite 4412; New York, NY 10118; Tel. (212) 695 9520; fax (212) 695 8229; web site <www.visitmalta.com>.

There are local tourist information bureaus at the following addresses on the islands.

Malta: Malta International Airport — arrivals lounge. Tel. 2169 9600; 1 City Arcades, City Gate, Valletta. Tel. 2123 7747.

Gozo: 1 Palm Street, Victoria (in Republic Square), Tel. 2155 8106; Mġarr Harbor. Tel. 2155 3343.

WEIGHTS AND MEASURES

Malta uses the metric system.

Distance

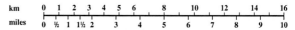

Temperature

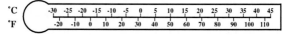

Length

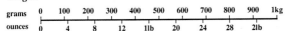

Weight

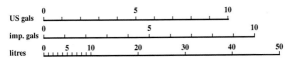

Fluid measures

WEB SITES

Web sites can be found in the contact details of individual attractions, hotels, and restaurants throughout this guide, however here are a few others that may help you to plan your trip.

<www.searchmalta.com>
<www.malta.co.uk>
<www.aboutmalta.com>
<www.holiday-malta.com

Y

YOUTH HOSTELS

The head office of the youth hostels association is:

       17 Triq Tal-Borġ (Tal-Borġ Street)
       Paola
       Malta
       Tel. 2169 3957

Recommended Hotels

Malta has a large range of hotels with a number of fine new 5-star establishments complementing hotels of other standards. Choices around the capital are limited since the resort areas have grown around the coastal bays — originally at St. Paul's and Bugibba, and Marsaxlokk, more recently at St. Julian's/Sliema just west of Valletta.

Prices are reasonable by European standards but some older hotels now look dated when compared with the dazzling new resorts. Smaller budget hotels may have more limited facilities, but all will be spotlessly clean.

Most large hotels will offer prices for B&B, half-board or full board, but with the range and good value of eateries around the island, it would be shame to limit yourself to the hotel restaurant for the whole of your stay.

Prices are generally quoted per person/per night with breakfast included. All rooms in 3-star establishments and above must have private facilities. Below this standard it is important to make inquiries about facilities before making a reservation. Prices rise during the summer months when it would be wise to make a reservation before you travel. A few hotels close during the winter but most have buoyant business at all times of year.

The following hotel recommendations are based on a combination of facilities and location. They are in the following price ranges for B&B per person in peak season.

€€€€€	above Lm40
€€€€	Lm25-40
€€€	Lm18-25
€€	Lm10-18
€	under Lm10

MALTA

(The international telephone code for Malta is 356.)

Corinthia Palace Hotel €€€€€ *De Paule Avenue, Attard BZN 05; Tel. 2144 0301; fax 2146 5713; <www.corinthiahotels.*

com>. Luxury resort hotel in the center of the island within sight of Mdina. The Corinthia Palace is the dowager of Malta hotels. Rooms have A/C, phone/computer point, hairdryer, mini-bar, safe, trouser press, radio and TV. Facilities on site include beach and watersports facilities at sister hotel in St. Julian's available to guests. 155 rooms. Major credit cards.

Hilton Malta €€€€€ *Portomaso, St. Julian's STJ 02; Tel. 2133 6201; fax 2134 1539; <www.hilton.com>.* This imposing new hotel sits on the headland at St. Julian's within easy reach of nightlife and fine local restaurants. Rooms have A/C, fax/modem, hairdryer, mini-bar, safe, trouser press, radio and TV. Facilities include five restaurants, three bars, shopping arcade, garden, gym, steam room, squash and tennis courts, indoor and outdoor pools, watersports and discotheque. Ramps throughout for the physically impaired. Two adapted rooms. 294 rooms. Major credit cards.

Le Méridien Phoenicia €€€€€ *The Mall, Floriana VLT 16; Tel. 2122 5241; fax 2123 5254; <www.lemeridien-phoenicia. com>.* This fine building (once the British officers' mess) has been tastefully upgraded and renovated in the 1990s. It is ideally placed, located only a few minutes stroll from the center of Valetta, and also the main bus station for the rest of the island. Rooms have A/C, phone, hairdryer, mini-bar, safe, trouser press, radio, and TV. Facilities include three restaurants, two bars, hairdressers, courtesy mini-bus (summer only), indoor and outdoor pool, mini-golf. 136 rooms. Major credit cards.

Radisson SAS Bay Point Resort €€€€€ *St. George's Bay, St. Julian's STJ 02; Tel. 2137 4894; fax 2137 4895; <www.island-hotels.com.mt>.* Situated on the edge of St. Julian's and Paceville within reach of the nightlife yet removed from it. Rooms have A/C, phone, mini-bar, coffee/tea, safe, trouser press, radio and TV. Facilities include four restaurants, five bars, gym, private beach, sauna, indoor and outdoor pool, tennis courts and powered watersports facilities. 252 rooms. Major credit cards.

Xara Palace €€€€ *Mirah il-Kunsill, Mdina MDN 02; Tel. 2145 0560; fax 2145 2612; <www.xarapalace.com.mt>.* A beautiful hotel located in the bastions of the medieval citadel. The rooms are furnished to the highest standards. A perfect place for a romantic getaway. Rooms have A/C, hairdryer, phone, mini-bar, safe, trouser press, radio, and TV. Facilities include two restaurants, bar, gym, whirlpool, sundeck, courtesy mini-bus. 17 suites. Major credit cards.

Coastline Hotel €€€ *Coast Road, Salina Bay SPB 08; Tel. 2157 3781; fax 2158 1104;<www.islandhotels.com>.* Large hotel overlooking Salina Bay, a couple of miles from Buġibba, and popular with tour groups from throughout Europe. Rooms have A/C, phone, mini-bar, coffee/tea, radio, and TV. Facilities include two restaurants, two bars, large gym, sauna, indoor and outdoor pools, courtesy mini-bus, tennis courts, whirlpool. 208 rooms. Major credit cards.

Corinthia Jerma Palace Hotel €€€ *Dawret it-Torri, Marsascala ZBR 10; Tel. 2163 3222; fax 2162 9485; <www.corinthiahotels.com>.* This large hotel is situated on the eastern tip of the island, a 10-minute walk out of Marsascala town. Rooms have A/C, phone, hairdryer, and TV. Facilities include restaurant, café, bar, indoor and outdoor pools, gym, private beach, sauna, tennis courts, watersports. Ramps and lifts in all public areas for the physically impaired. Two adapted rooms. 326 rooms. Major credit cards.

Gillieru Harbour €€€ *Church Square, St. Paul's Bay SPB 01; Tel. 2157 2720; fax 2157 2745.* Situated on the seafront next to a fishing harbor and the church square of St. Paul's Bay, it is ideal for strolling to the restaurants and bars. Rooms have A/C phone, mini-bar, safe, radio, and TV. Facilities include two restaurants, bar, pool, game room, watersports. 50 rooms. Major credit cards.

Grand Hotel Mercure Selmun Palace Coralia €€€€ *Selmun, Mellieħa SPB 10; Tel. 2152 1040; fax 2152 1159; <www.accor-hotels.com>.* Situated on a hill, high above Mellieħa Bay on the west of Malta, this hotel comprises a 17th-century castle with large but sympathetic modern addition. Rooms include A/C, phone, hairdryer, mini-bar, safe, radio and TV. Facilities include gourmet restaurant in castle chapel (Thurs, Fri, Sat), restaurant, bar, indoor and outdoor pools, game room, gym, private beach, courtesy mini-bus, tennis courts. 154 rooms, 6 suites in castle. Major credit cards.

Lapsi Hotel €€€ *Balluta Bay, St. Julian's STJ 15; Tel. 2137 8800; fax 2137 3227; <www.kemmunet.net.mt/lapsihotels>.* Overlooking the bay of Sliema and on the busy promenade, this new hotel puts you at the heart of the restaurant and night scene. Rooms have A/C, phone, hairdryer, mini-bar, safe, radio, and TV. Facilities include two restaurants, bar, indoor and outdoor swimming pools, gym, sauna, whirlpool, garden, courtesy mini-bus. 100 rooms. Major credit cards.

Mellieħa Bay Hotel €€€–€€€€ *Mellieħa Bay, Ghadira SPB 10; Tel. 2157 3841; fax 2157 6399.* This large hotel is situated across the street from the largest sandy beach on Malta. Bus routes to Valetta or Ċirkewwa for Gozo ferry, pass directly outside. A popular hotel with tour groups. Rooms have A/C, phone, radio. Facilities include restaurant, four bars, indoor and outdoor pools, tennis courts, watersports, garden, hairdresser, nightclub, TV lounge. 310 rooms. Major credit cards.

Paradise Bay Hotel €€€–€€€€ *Ċirkewwa SPB 10; Tel. 2157 3981; fax 2157 3115; <www.paradise_bay.com>.* A large hotel on the western tip of Malta overlooking the ferry dock for Gozo.

Popular dive facility here, but no restaurants or bars around the hotel. Rooms have A/C, phone, hairdryer, mini-bar, coffee/tea, radio, and TV. Facilities include two restaurants, two bars, private beach, indoor and outdoor swimming pools, tennis courts, watersports, hairdresser, shopping arcade. Elevators and room doors wide enough for wheelchair access. 217 rooms. Major credit cards.

Preluna Hotel and Towers €€€ *124 Tower Road, Sliema SLM 01; Tel. 2133 4001; fax 2134 2292; <www.preluna-hotel.com>.* This large hotel sits on the main coastal road at the eastern end of Sliema. It is popular with tour groups. Rooms have A/C, phone, mini-bar, hairdryer, safe, radio, and TV. Facilities include three restaurants, three bars, indoor and outdoor pools (outdoor pool across the street), gym, sauna, watersports. Ramps throughout the hotel. 280 rooms. Major credit cards.

The Suncrest Hotel €€€ *Qawra Coast Road, Qawra SPB 08; Tel. 2157 7101; fax 2157 5478; <www.suncresthotels.com>.* A large hotel overlooking the bay at Qawra with numerous facilities for guests but also within easy reach of lively Buġibba town with its clubs and bars. Rooms have A/C, phone, hairdryer, radio and TV. Facilities include six restaurants, four bars, discotheque, shopping arcade, indoor and outdoor pools, garden, gym, sauna, squash court, tennis court, watersports. Ramps throughout and all doors and elevators are wheelchair accessible. 434 rooms. Major credit cards.

Villa Rosa €–€€ *St. George's Bay, St. Julian's STJ 02; Tel. 2134 2707; fax 2131 6531.* This low-rise budget hotel sits well placed with luxury hotels all around and the restaurants and bars of St. Julian's within strolling distance. Rooms have phone, radio, and TV. Facilities include restaurant, bar, indoor and outdoor pools, gym, sauna, tennis court. 105 rooms. Major credit cards.

Castille Hotel €€ *348 St. Paul Street, Valletta VLT 01; Tel. 2124 3677; fax 2124 3677.* Close to Upper Barracca Gardens, this hotel is set in a converted 17th-century town house. Rooms have A/C, phone, radio and TV. Facilities include restaurant, coffee shop and bar. 39 rooms. Major credit cards.

The Limelight Hotel €€–€€€ *Triq G Centurjun, Buġibba SPB 03; Tel. 2157 2330; fax 2158 1270.* Hotel in the residential area of Buġibba town with lively restaurant, bar and club scene within walking distance. Five minutes walk to the sea front. Rooms have A/C phone, radio and TV. Facilities include restaurant, bar, pool and games room. 81 rooms. Major credit cards.

Grand Harbour Hotel € *47 Battery Street, Valletta VLT 01; Tel. 2124 6003; fax 2124 2219;* Small hotel with great harbor views. Rooms are small, clean, and have a TV. Facilities include restaurant and sundeck. 24 rooms. Major credit cards.

The Osborne Hotel €–€€€ *50 South Street, Valletta VLT 01; Tel. 2123 2127; fax 2123 2120; <www.osbornehotel.com>.* A well-appointed budget hotel in the center of the city. Rooms have A/C, phone, hairdryers and TV. Facilities include a pleasant bar, restaurant, small roof spa pool. 51 rooms. Prices are per room not per person. Major credit cards.

COMINO

Comino Hotels €€€ *Comino Island, SPB 10; Tel. 2152 9821; fax 2152 9826; <www.digigate.net/cominohotel>.* The only hotel on Comino which means that you only share the island with other guests after day-trippers disappear. Rooms have A/C hairdryer, phone, mini-bar, radio and TV. Facilities include two restaurants, pool, health club, tennis courts, games room, and hairdresser. Closed end of October–beginning of April each year. 95 rooms. Major credit cards.

GOZO

L'Imgarr €€€€ *Ghajnsielem GSM 104; Tel. 2156 0455; fax 2155 7589; <www.vol.net.mt/mgarr/imgarr1.htm>*. Built on a hillside overlooking the bay and port at Mġarr, the hotel is perfectly placed for day trips to Malta and Comino. Rooms have A/C hair dryer, phone, mini-bar, radio, TV, trouser press. Facilities include three restaurants, two pools, health club, sauna, whirlpool. 64 rooms and suites. Ramps throughout for the physically impaired. Major credit cards.

Ta' Cenc €€€€ *Sannat VTC 112; Tel. 2155 6819; fax 2155 8199*. In a country location but with private beach, Ta' Ċenċ is probably the best hotel in the islands. Rooms have A/C, phone, hairdryer, mini-bar, radio, and TV. Facilities include gourmet restaurant, bar, courtesy mini-bus, two pools (one adults-only), tennis courts, whirlpool and areas of land with dolmen and other remains to explore. 83 rooms and suites. Major credit cards.

St. Patrick's Hotel €€€ *Xatt ix-Xlendi, Xlendi VCT 115; Tel. 2156 2951; fax 2155 6598*. Beautifully located on the harbor in the picturesque cove at Xlendi, this new hotel takes design features from traditional buildings. Some rooms have windows and balconies overlooking the internal courtyard. The best rooms priced here have views over the bay. Rooms have A/C, phone, hair dryer, mini-bar, radio, TV. Facilities include restaurant, bar, splash pool, whirlpool. 45 rooms. Major credit cards.

Cornucopia Hotel €€€ *10 Ġnien Imrik Street, Xagħra VCT 110: Tel. 2155 6486; fax 2155 2910*. Pretty hotel in the center of the island, based on a converted farmhouse. Lots of atmosphere. Rooms have A/C, phone , mini-bar, trouser press, safe, hairdryer, radio, and TV. Facilities include two pools, restaurant, bar, games room, hairdresser. (also self-catering bungalows and converted farm houses). Major credit cards.

Recommended Restaurants

Malta is filled with inexpensive places to eat. Most are trattoria-style informal eateries, which serve a range of pasta and pizzas along with steaks and fish. A few serve the small range of native Maltese dishes, which are delicious. This is all washed down with Maltese wine — eminently drinkable and very good value. There are also many fast food outlets and snack bars so you should have little trouble finding something to suit you. For this recommended section, we have tried to source establishments that are just a little out of the ordinary either in the quality of food and service, the type of cuisine they offer, or in their location. Many restaurants offer set lunches and dinners in addition to an à-la-carte menu.

For some of the finer and smaller restaurants it would be wise to make a reservation, especially on weekends. Some restaurants open fewer days and shorter hours in winter; they may also close early out-of-season if they are not busy. Very few restaurants have a dress code, though you should check with the more expensive establishments. Slacks and sports jacket are usually fine.

Most restaurants will make a cover charge of 15c-30c per person — this will be indicated on your menu. Very few restaurants have separate "no smoking" areas. Sitting in the fresh air of a terrace is usually the best option for those who don't like cigarette smoke.

The following guidelines indicate the price of a three-course dinner per person without wine.

€€€€€	above LM15
€€€€	LM10-15
€€€	LM8-10
€€	LM5-8
€	below LM5

MALTA

Bacchus €€€ *Inguanez Alley, Mdina; Tel. 2145 4981.* Atmospheric restaurant set in the cellars of an old mansion down one of Mdina's narrow alleyways. Maltese and Italian cuisine along with grilled meats. Open daily 10am–midnight. Major credit cards.

Barracuda €€€–€€€€ *194 Main Street, St. Julian's; Tel. 2133 1817; <www.wgc-group.com>.* Pretty setting overlooking the bay at St. Julian's; fine Italian dining and fresh fish dishes. Open daily 7–10:30pm (closed Sunday in winter). Major credit cards.

Belfiore €€–€€€ *126 Main Street, St Julian's; Tel. 2134 4750.* Italian trattoria with pasta and pizzas. Worth a visit for the rooftop setting, above the traffic with good views across the bay and surrounding hotels. Open daily dinner 6–11pm. Major credit cards.

Bottega del Vino €€€ *At the Hilton Malta, Portomaso, St. Julian's; Tel. 2133 6201.* Open plan restaurant serving rustic Maltese and Italian dishes. Interesting anti-pasti, ample pasta choices, but also rabbit and Maltese sausage casserole, both of which are delicious. Open daily for lunch noon–3pm, dinner 6–11pm. Major credit cards.

Bouzouki €€€ *135 Spinola Road, St. Julian's; Tel. 2131 7127.* Greek tavern menu in up-market surroundings. Salads, souvlaki and slow cooked stews. Views across the harbor. Open daily lunch 12–2:30pm, dinner 6–11pm. Major credit cards.

Café de Paris €–€€ *Xatt is-Sajjieda, Marsaxlokk; Tel. 2165 0652.* Casual dining on the harbor front at Marsaxlokk. Fish brought in by the fleet is served here only hours later — grilled or fried. Prawns also a speciality. Some Maltese dishes and pizzas. Open daily 9am–10pm. Major credit cards.

The Carriage €€€€ *22-15 Valletta Buildings, South Street, Valletta; Tel. 2124 7828.* One of the finest restaurants in the city with silver service, beloved of Valletta businessmen at lunchtimes. Maltese and international dishes. Open for lunch Mon–Fri noon–3pm, dinner Fri–Sat 7:30–11pm. Major credit cards.

Corinthia Room Restaurant €€€€€ *At the Corinthia Palace Hotel, De Paule Avenue, Attard; Tel. 2144 0301.* Perhaps the most spectacular dining room on the island with food to match the décor, elegant and cultured. This is a place to dress up — a real occasion. European menu. Open daily for lunch 12:30–2:30pm, dinner 6:30–10:30pm. Reservations recommended. Major credit cards.

La Dolce Vita €€€–€€€€ *159 St. George's Road, St. Julian's; Tel. 2133 7036.* Renowned fish restaurant set on the bay at St. George's, very popular with locals and visitors so it's always busy. Reservation recommended for terrace tables. Open daily for lunch noon–2:30pm (summer only), dinner 7–11pm. Major credit cards.

Giannini €€€€ *23 Windmill Street, Valletta; Tel. 2127 3121.* This restaurant serves fine Italian and Maltese dishes, but although the food is delicious, many people come to enjoy the wonderful views over Marsamxett harbour. Lots of stairs to climb to get to the upper dining room. Open lunch daily noon–2:30pm, dinner Mon–Sat 6–10:30pm (Thurs–Sat in winter). Major credit cards.

Gillieru €€€ *66 Church Street, St. Paul's Bay; Tel. 2157 3480.* Large harbor-side restaurant (affiliated with the Gillieru Hotel) offering a good selection of fresh fish, Maltese and international dishes. The terrace is very popular and always busy in summer. Open daily lunch noon–2:30pm, dinner 7:30–11pm. Major credit cards.

Grabiel €–€€ *1 Mifsud Bonnici Street, Marsascala; Tel. 2168 4194*. Great little fish restaurant on the seafront at Marsascala, which serves whatever is freshly caught that day. You'll have to fight for a seat at weekends when families from around the island come here for lunch. Pasta Rizzi with fresh sea urchins is a speciality when in season. Some fish dishes sold by weight. Open daily 11am–10pm. Major credit cards.

Grapes €€ *1 Catacombs Street, Rabat; Tel. 2145 0483*. Small but cozy restaurant very close to the catacombs. It serves Maltese dishes and accompanies them with locally made wines. Open Mon–Sat lunch 11am–3pm, dinner 6:30–10pm (11pm Sat). Major credit cards.

Gusmana Navarra €–€€€ *28 St. Paul Street, Rabat; Tel. 2145 0638*. Easily located opposite St. Paul's Church, this restaurant is situated in an old house. On the first floor is a café/bar serving snacks; on the second a restaurant serving meat and fish dishes. Open Mon–Sat 6:30–10pm. Major credit cards.

It-Tokk €€€ *Qawra Coast Road, Qawra; Tel. 2157 7101*. Affiliated to the Suncrest Hotel but across the street from it, this restaurant specialises in Maltese dishes and fresh fish. Pride of place goes to the real *luzzu* fishing boat, which forms part of the serving area. Open daily lunch noon–2:30pm, dinner 6–10:30pm. Major credit cards.

L-Ghonnella €€€€ *Spinola Palace, St. Julian's; Tel. 2134 1027*. Set in the cellar of this palace built in 1688, the L-Ghonella has atmosphere, a good menu of Maltese and Italian Milenese dishes, and a fine wine list. Elegant dining. Open daily except Tues, dinner only 6–10pm. Major credit cards.

Little China Restaurant €€€ *Triq il-Halel, Buġibba; Tel. 2157 2286*. Of three or four Chinese restaurants, this one has a good range of dishes nicely cooked and presented. Ample portions. Open daily 5pm–midnight, Sun lunch 11:30am–3pm. Major credit cards.

Lulu €€€–€€€€ *31 Church Street, St. Julian's; Tel. 2137 7211.* An intimate restaurant with only eight tables, Lulu serves fine Italian cuisine. Pretty décor and understated music. Open Mon–Sat, dinner only 7–11pm. Major credit cards.

Marianna's Tex-Mex €€€ *132 Tower Road, Sliema; Tel. 2131 8943.* All the usual suspects in this cantina-style informal restaurant. Chili, surf and turf, chicken wings and tacos. Open daily 11am–11pm. Major credit cards.

Sumatra Restaurant €€€ *139 Spinola Road, St. Julian's; Tel. 2131 0991.* Excellent Malaysian, Singaporean and Indonesian food in this modern restaurant just off the main street in St. Julian's. Open Mon–Sat, dinner only 7–11pm.

TGI Fridays €€–€€€ *Il-Fortizza, Tower Road, Sliema; Tel. 2133 6908.* This chain of restaurants sells American-style burgers, steaks and finger foods, but none of their outlets is as spectacular as this imposing 17th-century fort set on the seafront at Sliema. Informal and relaxed, but the music can be loud. Open daily 11am–11pm. Major credit cards.

Trattoria Campanella €€–€€€ *15 Windmill Street, Valletta; Tel. 2125 0837.* Pretty restaurant set in arched stone rooms very near Hastings Gardens. Pizzas, pastas, and grilled meats. Open for lunch daily noon–3pm, dinner Mon–Sat 6–10:30pm. Major credit cards.

Palazzo Notabile €€–€€€ *Triq Villegaignon, Mdina; Tel. 2145 4625.* Pizza, pasta, sandwiches, and burgers in the courtyard of an old Mdina palace, linked to the Medieval Times Adventure attraction. Open daily 10am–10pm. Major credit cards.

Piccolo Padre €€–€€€ *195 Main Street, St. Julian's; Tel. 2134 4875.* Sister restaurant to the Barracuda and situated below it, Piccolo Padre serves great pizza and pasta in a rustic informal setting. Maltese and Gozitan ingredients add extra interest to some dishes. Some tables overlook the bay. Open daily 7–11pm. Major credit cards.

Vino Veritas €€–€€€ *59 Sir Adrian Dingle Street, Sliema. Tel. 2132 4273.* An exceptionally good trattoria run by amiable folks — relaxed atmosphere but never too noisy. All the usual menu items and Italian/Maltese wine choices. The portions are huge, so bring your appetite. Open Tues–Sat, lunch noon–2:30pm, dinner 6:30–11:30pm (the kitchen closes, but the restaurant stays open until the last customers leaves). Major credit cards.

GOZO

Gelmus €€€–€€€€ *56 Foreman Street, Victoria (Rabat); Tel. 2155 8047.* French and European cuisine in this old stone house. There is a pretty terrace for outside dining. Just a 10-minute walk from central Victoria. Open Tue–Sun, lunch noon–3pm, dinner 6–11pm. Major credit cards.

Jeffrey's €€€ *10 Triq el-Gharb, San Lawrenz; Tel. 2156 1006.* Situated next door to Gozo Glass, Jeffrey's is a well-established restaurant with tables outside at the rear, offering dishes made with whatever is in season. Rabbit and fish appear regularly. There are always pasta dishes on the menu. Open daily 7–10pm. Major credit cards.

Restaurant Pizzeria Il-Kartell €€€ *Triq il-Forn, Marselforn; Tel. 2155 6918.* Popular restaurant set in an old Gozitan building on the harbor front. A good selection of fish and meat dishes in addition to pizzas. Live music in the summer. Open daily, lunch 11:45am–3pm dinner 7–11pm. Major credit cards.

Il Terrazzo €€€–€€€€ *St. Simon Street, Xlendi; Tel 2156 2992;* *<www.gozo.com/terrazzo>.* Pretty restaurant set above the bay in Xlendi. Attention to detail in the décor and table setting, and the food makes it worth a visit. Italian menu and fresh fish dishes which change with the catch. Open daily, lunch noon–3pm, dinner 6:30–11pm. Major credit cards.

Republic Restaurant and Trattoria €€–€€€ *24 Marina St, Marsalforn; Tel. 2155 6800.* Authentic trattoria food — pizza and pastas. Good atmosphere and good value. Open Tue–Sun, lunch 11am–3pm, dinner 6:30–10:30pm. Major credit cards.

Il-Carrubo €€€€ *Ta' Ċenċ Hotel, Sannat; Tel. 2155 6819.* Gourmet restaurant serving Italian and Gozitan menu, accompanied by fresh seasonal vegetables from the hotel garden. Fresh pasta made for lunch and dinner. Fine wine list from around the world. Beautiful courtyard setting. Live music each night in summer. Open daily, lunch noon–2pm, dinner 7–9:30pm. Reservation recommended. Major credit cards.

Ta' Rikardu € *4, Triq il-Fosos, Citadella (the Citadel), Victoria (Rabat); Tel. 2155 5953.* Set above a souvenir shop beside the Cathedral, Ta' Rikardu has only one dish on the menu, Gozitan cheese, fresh Gozitan salad — olives, bell peppers, onions, tomatoes, served with fresh, crusty bread, and home-produced wine. The platters can be shared with a group or ordered per person. The wine is included in the price. Open daily, lunch only noon–2:30pm. Major credit cards.

INDEX